MATERIALIZING POVERTY

Anthropology of Daily Life Series

Series Editors:

Jessica Chelekis, University of Southern Denmark, jessi@sam.sdu.dk

Richard Wilk, Indiana University, wilkr@indiana.edu

Orvar Löfgren, University of Lund, Orvar.Lofgren@kultur.lu.se

Cultural anthropologists often touch on daily life as part of their studies of other topics, but anthropological scholarship on everyday life is often scattered across works concentrating on other themes. Meanwhile, daily life is becoming an increasingly popular topic of investigation in a variety of other fields of inquiry. By focusing on daily life, this series combines elements from fields as diverse as American Studies, Cultural Geography, European Ethnology, Sociology, Anthropology, Archaeology, Museum Studies, Communication and Culture, Consumer Research, Technology and Society, and Consumption Studies. The **Anthropology of Daily Life** series presents investigations into particular elements of everyday life, focusing on how people use and engage with objects, as well as the practices, activities, and social spaces of daily life. This examination into daily life offers profound insight into the connections between how people see the world and how they act.

Books in the Series

Materializing Poverty: How the Poor Transform Their Lives, by Erin B. Taylor

MATERIALIZING POVERTY

How the Poor Transform Their Lives

Erin B. Taylor

ROWMAN & LITTLEFIELD
Lanham • Boulder • New York • Toronto • Plymouth, UK

Published Rowman & Littlefield
4501 Forbes Boulevard, Suite 200, Lanham, Maryland 20706
www.rowman.com

10 Thornbury Road, Plymouth PL6 7PP, United Kingdom

British Library Cataloguing in Publication Information Available

Library of Congress Cataloging-in-Publication Data
Taylor, Erin B.
Materializing poverty : how the poor transform their lives / Erin B. Taylor.
pages cm
Includes bibliographical references and index.
ISBN 978-0-7591-2421-9 (cloth : alk. paper)—ISBN 978-0-7591-2422-6 (electronic)
1. Poor—Dominican Republic—Santo Domingo—Social conditions. 2. Material culture—Dominican Republic—Santo Domingo. 3. Squatter settlements—Dominican Republic—Santo Domingo. 4. Poverty—Dominican Republic—Santo Domingo. 5. Social values—Dominican Republic—Santo Domingo. I. Title.
HN219.S2T39 2013
305.5'69097293'75—dc23
2013032736

∞™ The paper used in this publication meets the minimum requirements of American National Standard for Information Sciences Permanence of Paper for Printed Library Materials, ANSI/NISO Z39.48-1992.

Printed in the United States of America

To my parents, Paul and Rosemary Taylor, for embarking me upon this path, and to my husband, Gawain Lynch, for accompanying me to its end

CONTENTS

ACKNOWLEDGMENTS

My first and greatest thanks go to my doctoral supervisor, Diane Austin-Broos, who I stumbled across by an extraordinary stroke of luck. Diane patiently and firmly guided me through the corpus of Caribbean anthropology, always encouraging me to find my own voice, an approach that I appreciate profoundly. Her supervision instilled in me great enthusiasm for anthropology and my own research topic.

My second thanks go to Linda Connor for getting me fixated on anthropology as an undergraduate. Her courses in medical anthropology and ethnographic film, and her supervision of my final-year thesis, cemented my decision to major in anthropology and continue on to postgraduate studies in anthropology.

Much of the research for this book was carried out between 2004 and 2005 for my doctoral degree at the University of Sydney, funded by the University Postgraduate Scheme (co-funded with the Faculty of Arts), the Carlyle Greenwell Bequest, and the Postgraduate Research Support Scheme. In 2009, as a lecturer at the University of Sydney, I received a grant from the Faculty of Arts to do follow-up research.

This book was written during my employment as a Postdoctoral Research Fellow at the Social Science Institute (ICS) at the University of Lisbon, funded by the Foundation for Science and Technology (FCT). The ICS has been very generous in permitting me time to think and write. I would especially like to thank my supervisor, José Sobral, for his encouragement and support. Portugal has been an amazing host country and provided perfect conditions for the production of knowledge in a beautiful and inspiring environment.

Over the years, my academic mentors have been generous and indispensable. Constance Sutton at New York University visited me in the field and provided early feedback on my writing. Kevin Yelvington at the University of South Florida and Donald Robotham at City University New York helped me develop contacts in the field. Heather Horst at RMIT in Melbourne has been a valuable friend and colleague, offering advice on everything under the sun. Daniel Miller has been more helpful than he probably realizes, prompting me to decide how to pull this book together as well as assisting me in getting it published!

In Santo Domingo many people assisted me in finding my way around the city and its history. They include the vice-rector of the Pontifica Universidad Católica Madre y Maestra, Radhamés Mejía, the Jesuit priests from the Centro de Estudios Sociales (especially Padres Mario Serrano, Javier Vidal, and Delsen Innocent), FLACSO, and **CO-PADEBA**. Jorge Cela, Jesuit priest and general coordinator of Fé y Alegría, read my dissertation and provided very useful and insightful feedback.

In La Ciénaga, I was fortunate to be immediately adopted by Adela Veloz Cruz and her extended family, with whom I spent countless hours drinking *café dulce* (sweet coffee) and *hablando vaina* (gossiping). Bélgica helped me connect with the community, and Carmencita took me under her wing. *Muchas gracias también a mis vecinos en Respaldo Clarín, toda la gente de la iglesia, CODECI, la Junta de Vecinos, y los niños del barrio. Muchísimas gracias a Yoselyn Espinal, Marco Quiroz Rodriguez, y Felix Quiroz Rodriguez*, who, besides supporting me with their friendship, have also worked as my research assistants at various stages over the past eight years.

I wish to thank my parents, Paul and Rosemary Taylor, for teaching me intellectual curiosity and an interest in social justice, which sparked my anthropological thinking and prompted me to search out this research topic. I appreciate your support and nice cups of tea over the years. To my brother, Glenn, and my sister, Belinda, may we always be ridiculous together. Thanks to my friends Dmitri Kavetski, Gloria Kavetski, Isabelle Rivoal, Aimee Tubnor, Barbara Baumann, and Todd Sanderson for your support. A special thanks to Jason Tampake for our many enabling discussions in front of the fireplace. Vanessa Kurz was fantastic in taking photos for this book at a moment's notice. An extra-special thanks to Barbara Vreede for her comments on the all-but-final version of this book.

Finally, fervent thanks to my domestic goddess, Gawain, whose invaluable insights into this book's subject matter were shared over amazing dinners that he prepared himself. Gawain also painstakingly read several versions of this book, which had the interesting side-effect of spawning the PopAnth website! Because one massive project at a time is never enough. May there be many more collective mammoth endeavors in our future.

INTRODUCTION

The Wealth of Poverty

It is an unusually clear summer's day in Santo Domingo. Taking advantage of the break in the torrential tropical rain, Felix is adding concrete bricks to his parents' house. Already under construction for over forty years, the house will never be finished, but it bears no resemblance to the wood and tin structure that his parents, Cristino and Maria, originally bought for fifty pesos in 1972. In fact, it has transformed remarkably since I first visited the family in January 2005. Back then, the house was in a state of flux. Wooden walls were being slowly replaced with concrete blocks, the family kept changing their mind about where doors should be located, and the furniture would be moved around to accommodate the changing shape of the house. The construction of the house wasn't just a practical process for the family; it was a community event. Every afternoon, visitors would gather on the porch to drink sweet coffee and contribute their opinions on the optimal design for the house, both for immediate use and for the family's future growth. In a squatter settlement, builders, architects, and government regulations have little to do with shaping houses. Instead, families and friends build homes with love and a lot of *inventando* (inventing).

To this day, Cristino does not have legal title to his land. While he can prove ownership of his house, he is squatting at the mercy of the state. Yet Cristino does not sit and fret about whether he will lose his home. Much to his disappointment, he was not among those who were relocated to new apartments in the evictions of 1977 and 1991. Cristino would have liked to have taken his family away from this *barrio*, with its frequent flooding, landslides, mosquitoes, diseases, and lack of services, but his dream never came true. Nor does it look like eventuating any time soon for his eldest son, Felix, who is raising his own young family in a house that he built in his parents' backyard. His younger brother, Marco, also remains at home. He is helping to finish his parents' house so that he can construct a second floor that will be his own. This family's story is repeated throughout Santo Domingo's barrios, as new generations with little socioeconomic mobility build on the material legacy of their parents.

A few thousand kilometers away, somewhere in the United States, a family is being dispossessed from their home. Since the subprime housing crisis rocked markets and lives in late 2007, more than 3 million mortgages have been foreclosed in the United States (Abel and Tracy 2012). The global financial crisis (GFC), officially bracketed as running its course from 2007 to 2010, is not over for homeowners: a further 2 million foreclosures are in process (ibid.). With a rough average of three people per household in the United States, this represents a total of 15 million people who have lost their home and been forced to seek alternative accommodation. In the first two years, they were more likely than not to be from families that were low income before the GFC, but since unemployment hit a high of 10 percent in October 2009, many are from middle-class backgrounds (Carey 2012). Black families are disproportionately represented in the count of the displaced, as they were more likely to be the subject of "predatory" lending practices and granted a subprime loan with a higher interest rate, resulting in a struggle to pay off mortgages as interest rates rose and times became tougher (Rugh and Massey 2010).

The subprime mortgage crisis and subsequent foreclosures sent shockwaves through Middle America. All of a sudden, impoverishment was not just something that could happen to the unwise and unprepared: rather, an ever-widening array of people were susceptible to crisis. This was not just a concern for economic outcomes: by any measure, losing one's home is an emotionally fraught experience. Our homes, more than any other site, are where we have autonomy to express our identities and create our familial lives. They are also supposed to provide us with security, which made the extent of house repossessions all the more troubling. To express this new feeling of collective crisis—of so many people being at the mercy of the vicissitudes of the global economy—Americans and many others around the world nicknamed themselves "the 99 percent."

In contrast, most of the large banks that were in crisis (with the exception of Lehman Brothers, which was liquidated) were bailed out by governments. They had been deemed "too big to fail," a term that was first popularized during the Reagan era of the early 1980s, referring to the idea that some financial institutions are so large that allowing them to collapse would send the economy into a tailspin. Against the tenets of liberal ideology, then, these institutions were granted rescue packages, and more regulation was put in place in an attempt to prevent a repeat of the crisis. Anthropologist Gillian Tett, in her analysis of the events leading up to the GFC, puts a slightly different slant on their importance, stating, "Quite apart from whether they were 'too *big* to fail,' they were too interconnected to ignore" (Tett 2009, 224–25). She argues that it was not the size of the institutions' portfolios per se that precipitated the crisis, but the ways in which they traded among themselves, which led to an accumulation of calculation errors and sparked a domino effect when those errors came to light.

This interconnectivity was not something that operated among homeowners, who had vertical relations with lenders rather than horizontal relations with each other—at least, until the 99 percent movement began. That is, there was no representative or advocacy body through which they could lobby for their interests, no shared responsibility or risk, no shared identity. They were spatially dispersed and socially disparate. An atomized group, they could not leverage commonality to protect their wealth.

It is strange, then, that just a few hundred kilometers away, in the Caribbean, Dominican squatters seem to be better off than Americans, at least where housing security and cooperation are concerned. With no land title and no property rights, residents of Santo Domingo's squatter settlements stand no risk of their homes being repossessed by the bank, because they have no mortgages. Nor do they risk their homes being repossessed by the state, for they have safety in numbers: having settled slowly but persistently over the years, there are now tens of thousands of people in the barrios. Much of the land they occupy, especially around the river near the city center, has a high market value. But the state would not risk a political scandal to dislodge them; nor does it have the capital necessary to relocate them all. Squatter residents face a plethora of other problems, but they have a security of residence that is far superior to that of many people in developing countries. Like the largest banks, their community is "too big to fail."

This idea that squatters may have something in common with large banks that middle Americans do not may seem preposterous, yet it speaks to the complicated nature of wealth and poverty. Poverty is not an absolute condition; it is not even necessarily an objective condition. While there are certainly people who live in abject poverty—in which their lives and health are threatened—most of our judgments regarding who is poor and who is not are subjective and relative. Not only do people around the world have vastly different ways of thinking about their own wealth and the wealth of others, but the experience of loss must also be taken into account, as the process of impoverishment—of becoming poorer than one was before—can intensify one's feeling of being poor even if one is wealthier than average.

Why do subjectivity and relativity matter? I argue that when we label people as "poor" without also investigating their situation as it is seen through their own eyes, we do them a great disservice. As James Holston has pointed out about Brazilian favelas, "poor" people simply do not sit around in a hopeless situation, waiting for someone (state, banks, NGOs, companies) to solve their problems. Rather, they actively construct their lives with the resources that are available to them, including found materials, help from neighbors, bought supplies, and a lot of inventando. Far from being helpless and inactive, poor people command a great deal of "competence and knowledge in the production and consumption of [modern goods]" (Holston 1991, 462). When we look closely at how the poorer segments of society use material and social resources—their wealth—we are forced to rethink our assumptions about poverty as lived experience.

Poverty is generally defined as a lack of material resources, or the possession of the wrong kinds of resources (rags rather than designer clothing, tin houses rather than brick). However, the relationships that poor people have with their possessions are not just about deprivation. Like everyone else, poor people use material forms to creatively construct their personal identities and communities, and to transform their futures. Indeed, Daniel Miller suggests that consumption may have heightened importance for the poorer segments of society because they depend heavily on the few things they possess in order to create their social identities in the face of an alienating world (Miller 2001). Their relationship to homes, clothes, and other material goods may be more complex and nuanced precisely because the range of goods they have access to is limited.

This book challenges common ideas about poverty. Most ethnographies of poor communities focus on the struggles of living with limited resources or the creative ways in which poor people use their personal possessions. They only rarely investigate how the relationships that poor people have with material things can transform their lives, both individually and collectively. History tells us that human social and cultural life depends on material forms for its expression, regardless of whether we are rich or poor, and that this holds true across time and space. Hunters and gatherers, slum dwellers, and fishing communities alike create artifacts and homes that express their social relations and their individuality in ways that cannot be reduced to an expression of poverty. However, materiality (and the category of "the poor") is also very much part of how inequalities are reproduced. Lack of resources creates very real constraints on life chances, such as not being able to pay for education or not owning the right clothes for a job interview. My analysis pays tribute to the sufferings of the poor, while exploring aspects of poverty that cannot be explained in terms of oppression or resistance alone.

My empirical evidence centers on my fieldwork in the Dominican Republic between 2004 and 2012. I lived for a year in an infamous squatter settlement called La Ciénaga, located on the banks of the Ozama River in Santo Domingo. Settled in the 1960s after the death of the dictator Rafael Leonidas Trujillo, La Ciénaga houses approximately 18,000 people living on 35.71 hectares, about 504.06 residents per hectare (Tejeda 2000, 21). Not a single household has a legal land title, but the everyday persistence of families in building their homes, sometimes over decades, has literally cemented their residence in the community. However, the barrio is also materially poor, evident in its many shacks, poor services and utilities, higher risk of natural disasters, low wages, and nonexistence of land titles.

Despite these constraints, residents of La Ciénaga find that their material existence enables them as much as it constrains them, and they employ all sorts of creative processes and strategies to solve everyday problems and, over a few decades, radically transform the community in which they live. La Ciénaga (literally meaning "the Swamp") may be a ***barrio marginado*** (marginalized barrio), but it is not stagnant as its name suggests. Due to the efforts of its residents, the community does not even remotely resemble the mud-stricken, isolated outpost that Cristino found when he moved there in 1972. The everyday engagements of residents with materiality have generated social change and transformed the status of the community over the past few decades. Today it is a fully urban community, with paved streets, electricity, parks, and an increasing amount of pride.

In fact, the ways in which residents think of themselves has also changed since I first arrived in the barrio. In a survey of three hundred residents that I conducted in November 2005, in response to the open question "What social class do you think you belong to?" 69 percent replied "*pobre*" (poor), 21 percent replied "*clase bajo*" (lower class), 1 percent replied "*clase media baja*" (lower-middle class), and 14 percent replied "*clase media*" (middle class). When I repeated the survey in November 2009, the results were strikingly different. Four years on, just 19 percent of respondents described themselves as poor, while 50 percent described themselves as lower class, 15 percent as lower-middle class, and 21 percent as middle class. Residents had shifted away from viewing themselves as "poor" to instead viewing themselves as being on the bottom of a class rung. Moreover, 21 percent more residents now defined themselves as lower-middle class or middle class. Materially and psychologically, residents were reaping the benefits of the barrio's slow transformation over four decades.

According to the World Bank (2013), the Dominican Republic has been one of the fastest-growing economies over the last decade, with economic growth averaging 9.5 percent from 2005 to 2007. The development of the tourist industry and the construction of industrial free zones (**IFZ**s) from the late 1960s shifted the focus of the economy from agriculture to services and assisted in the distribution of economic growth in diverse sites around the country. From 2005 to 2011, the gross national income by purchasing power parity (GNI [PPP]) per capita increased from US$6,020 to US$9,420 (World Bank 2013). In the same period, the number of people living below the national poverty line decreased from 47.8 percent to 40.4 percent. In urban areas, levels of poverty have consistently been slightly lower than the national average but have decreased more slowly, from 42.8 percent in 2005 and 36.5 percent in 2011. The benefits of this transformation are not even: nearly 40 percent of citizens still live below the poverty line, and the gap between the wealthy and the poor is maintained through the monopolization of social, cultural, and economic capital (Bourdieu 1986). However, there is little doubt that life has improved for many poor Dominicans over the last few decades. Overcoming poverty is achieved through actions on numerous fronts: the productive social and economic activities of citizens, changing state policy, and the repositioning of the Dominican Republic in the global economy. In this book I hope to demonstrate the crucial role that individual and collective manipulation of material forms and their social meanings plays in achieving this transformation.

CHAPTER OUTLINE

This book is divided into six chapters. Chapter 1 develops a framework for thinking through what poverty is as an analytical concept. I discuss how our measures of poverty relate to our ideas about ourselves as workers and consumers. I then show how examining our relationships with different kinds of material things—possessions, spaces, and the human body—can help us to understand poverty as a lived experience, not just as an abstract concept. Finally, I describe La Ciénaga, a squatter settlement in Santo Domingo whose poverty and illegality are the very reasons why its residents have been able to successfully migrate to the city and carve out a new kind of life for themselves and their children.

More than any other possession or motivation, the ability to construct one's own home is the reason why La Ciénaga exists. Chapter 2 describes residents' attempts to achieve material security and a measure of control over their social environment. The need to construct housing illegally and without professional assistance is indicative of residents' poverty, and residents are constrained by hard limits, including dangerous living conditions and lack of funds to buy building materials. However, the lifelong process of building one's own home (what James Holston [1991] terms "autoconstruction") on untitled land is also a compelling example of a positive trade-off gained by living in a stigmatized neighborhood. Relative freedom from government intervention means that residents can build and furnish their homes over many years, construct a local society of their own design, and eventually provide themselves with a measure of security from natural disasters and economic crises. As we will see, the freedoms they gain are not limited to building concrete things: they also literally construct a community in which their family members live close by, allowing for a level of public socializing that many middle-class Dominicans lament is disappearing from their lives as the nation retreats indoors in response to crime.

No account of the materiality of poverty could hold without an analysis of property possession and the violence that underlies it. In chapter 3 I explore how residents have maintained a precarious hold on those material accoutrements that are so central to their ability to create a community. Faced with two mass evictions and a four-year blockade by the military, residents have fought prominent battles with the state over issues of land rights and resettlement. During these conflicts, there has rarely been consensus among barrio residents as to what the outcome of these battles should be. Some people were desperate to leave the barrio; others did not wish to be dislodged. Yet one thing persists: new people continue to move into the barrios, and existing residents continue to construct their houses, despite the efforts of the state to halt the process of urbanization. This persistence of need has rendered the barrio as, essentially, "too big to ignore": the state can no longer reclaim the land for development, because relocating its thousands of residents is an economic and political impossibility. It is these everyday efforts to construct the barrio, far more than any organized political resistance, that has made the barrio into a permanent part of the city. Their persistence in occupying the land is a political act in itself: residents have ignored official instructions and instead sought progress in a fashion that they consider accessible to them. That is to say, the politics of squatting—its struggles and ultimate triumph—is borne not of ideology and political coordination, but of everyday material practices constituted over time and in space.

Chapter 4 turns to the role that religion plays in assisting people to interpret the present and dream of the future. I discuss the centrality of organized religion to local ideas of progress, and the tension between improving the material environment versus placing one's hopes for betterment in the afterlife. Some residents believe that the barrio can be transformed into an ideal modern community through widening streets, demolishing shacks, creating parks, and so on. But many other residents believe that there is no hope for the barrio, due to its inherent corruption, ongoing national crises, and even the increase of "wickedness" around the globe. Chronically poor and stigmatized in the media, the only chance of improvement is to escape, by either moving elsewhere or tolerating bad conditions until one is finally rewarded with the second coming of Christ. I demonstrate how even hopes for the future that are based on leaving the material world altogether (this life is bad, but I will be rewarded in the afterlife) are expressed and practiced through material objects. Examining the material practices of religion can illuminate why some people believe in material change, yet others do not.

Chapter 5 serves as a counterbalance to chapter 2's optimistic stance, showing how the freedoms gained through barrio residence are constrained by the social stigma held against the barrio and its residents by the media and the general public. A combination of La Ciénaga's poverty and visibility, coupled with Santo Domingo's rising crime rates, has led to the barrio becoming a master symbol of national failure. A widely accepted spatial dualism defines the city's high ground as respectable and moral, contra the spaces that the barrios occupy in swampy land around the river, whose inferior material qualities lend themselves to interpretations of the barrio's residents as immoral. I examine ten years of media reports about La Ciénaga and its surrounding neighborhoods to show how these poor barrios are conflated in the city's social imaginaries as dangerous and immoral, despite the fact that they differ from one another in significant ways. My analysis compares the views of outsiders and insiders to demonstrate how barrio residents come to terms with their stigmatization and attempt to distance themselves from actual crime and representations of crime.

In chapter 6 I describe how, reluctantly locked into place, residents use materiality to create their own personal identities and make value judgments about their neighbors. Residents of La Ciénaga reproduce the city's spatial dualism within the confines of their own barrio, conflating the level of material development of different barrio spaces with judgments of individuals' moral value. Within this identity politics, people attempt to carve out identities for themselves, whether as respectable homeowners, streetwise people marked out by ownership of mass-consumption goods, self-styled politicians attempting to transform the barrio, or as Haitian immigrants attempting to gain acceptance despite centuries of **antihaitianismo** (anti-Haitianism). Yet barrio residents are not simply pitted against one another: they also draw upon national identity categories that unite more than they divide. This normative value system provides a way for barrio residents to oppose their marginalization and claim a mainstream position in Dominican society. This core identity may be a fiction, but it creates a common narrative that residents draw upon as they make meaning of their lives and move forward into the future.

Finally, the book's coda shifts back to a comparison of the Dominican Republic with Haiti to demonstrate how material poverty and social values are context specific and change over time. I argue that a polyvalent understanding of poverty can help us to understand the vastly different ways in which poverty and social hierarchy are experienced around the world. The experiences and values associated with marginalization are necessarily expressed through our relationship with the object world. Better understanding the materiality of everyday poverty and the world at large can assist in unmasking how poverty is produced, reproduced, and transformed.

I

MORE THAN ARTIFACTS

The Materiality of Poverty

On March 18, 2011, I arrived in Santo Domingo after a nine-hour bus ride from Port-au-Prince. Entering the Dominican capital was a shock to the system after spending two months in a Haitian disaster zone. Newly painted glass and concrete buildings stood in neat rows, nestled in tropical foliage. Well-dressed pedestrians flowed sparsely and smoothly along the evenly paved sidewalks. It struck me that a parent could actually push a stroller along one of these paths with no difficulty at all. Luxury vehicles were directed along well-maintained roads by instructional signs and physical barriers. It was eerily quiet. Santo Domingo appeared to my Haiti-filled senses to be a strange, shining example of order, governance, and care. It looked, I thought at the time, like California.

I don't know what shocked me more: to find that Haiti and the Dominican Republic are materially so distinct, or to find that my new impression of Santo Domingo was so different from when I first arrived in September 2004. Back then, Santo Domingo looked—and was—markedly run down. Bent signposts, a plethora of litter, and potholes large enough to swallow entire families were the order of the day. As a result, when I first visited Port-au-Prince in January 2011, it felt oddly familiar. Although I knew that Haiti and the Dominican Republic are significantly different places, I could not shake the feeling of being back in Santo Domingo. Economically, the Dominican Republic is far wealthier than its neighbor; culturally, the two nations differ in their linguistic and religious practices, and politically, the Dominican Republic has been stable for longer. Yet despite these differences, and the damage caused by the earthquake, Santo Domingo and Port-au-Prince retain a common aesthetic. Port-au-Prince's concrete buildings painted tropical colors, recycled or polyester clothing, people playing dominoes on the street, and smells of food and diesel in particular triggered my sense of being in *la dominicana*. I could intellectualize the differences, yet my body was telling me that the two cities are materially and experientially similar.

Few people would have agreed with me. Dominicans, Haitians, and foreigners alike draw strong contrasts between Haiti and the Dominican Republic, mostly along axes of security/violence, order/disorder, black/brown, stable/unstable. Ironically, though, some of the differences they identify turn out to be similarities after all. One captain in the United Nations Stabilization Mission in Haiti (MINUSTAH) was stunned when I showed him photos of the squatter settlement in Santo Domingo that is the subject of this book. "This is in Santo Domingo?" he exclaimed. "But it looks like Cité du Soleil!" He knew Santo Domingo well, but he had no idea that there are areas with a level of poverty that rivals Haiti's most infamous slums.

Like their Haitian counterparts, many residents of Santo Domingo's barrios are at risk of some of the worst effects of destitution. Proximity to the Ozama River and poor sanitation mean that infectious diseases such as typhoid and dengue fever break out regularly. Dominican newspapers assert that the barrios were the epicenter of an outbreak of cholera in May 2011, implicitly drawing parallels between their poverty and that of Haiti. In August 2008, a landslide caused by tropical storm Gustav killed eight people in the slums, and many more people are living in dangerous and uncomfortable conditions. Barrio residents recognize—and appreciate—the material improvement programs that their governments have undertaken in recent years, but change is slow and insufficient. Yet residents of Santo Domingo's squatter settlements share with their compatriots a strong view that they are distinct from Haitians in every way. This is not merely an illusion: life in the Dominican Republic is generally far more secure than life in Haiti. Nevertheless, poverty, in both its abject and relative forms, is present across the breadth of the island.

Today, much has visibly changed in both cities: Santo Domingo for the better, and Port-au-Prince for the worse. In Santo Domingo, there is far less rubbish on the streets, thanks to a government program employing people to pick up litter by hand. Maintenance and construction projects have improved the aesthetics and utility of transport routes, and colorful children's playgrounds bring life to numerous plazas—not just in the city center, but in poor barrios as well. The picture is starkly different in Port-au-Prince. Fourteen months after a 7.0 magnitude earthquake devastated the Haitian capital, piles of rubble and condemned buildings still dominate the built environment. Streets are impossibly congested and the traffic appears to invent its own rules in a semi-random fashion. Every park hosts a camp of internally displaced persons, and the entire city looks like one giant open-air market, with vendors (mainly women) selling clothes, food, and electronics on the sidewalks. Most luxury cars are utility vehicles owned by NGOs, reflecting in a not-too-subtle manner their view of the need for practicality in Haiti, and negating the possibility of leisure. Astonishingly, a handful of overtly ostentatious Porsche Cayenne and BMW X-Series cars prowl the streets of Port-au-Prince, defying the reality of the city's potholes, kidnappings, and abject poverty.

My experiences on the island of Hispaniola, across time and place, left me puzzled as to how we can define *poverty*. In comparison with Haiti, the Dominican Republic seems wealthy; in comparison with the United States, it seems poor. If poverty is so dependent on comparison, how can we ever say anything definitive about it? Poverty is also relative at the level of the individual and the group: a person may be considered poor within their own social group, but well off in another. Similarly, one group may be considered wealthy within their own city, but poor by the standards of people living elsewhere. What counts as wealth may differ from one culture to the next. Yet poverty is real: access to resources shapes the choices that one can make, and a lack of resources can lead to physical harm or death. How people experience and classify poverty involves a complex interplay of the resources that people can access, and the status attached to those resources.

In this chapter I tease out a framework for thinking through what poverty is as an analytical concept. I discuss how our most common ways of measuring poverty draw upon our socioeconomic status and our roles as producers and consumers of goods. I suggest that to understand how poverty is produced through social and material means, it can be useful to examine different kinds of material things—namely, objects, spaces, and bodies—and how people use them to achieve different things in life. I then introduce La Ciénaga, a squatter settlement whose materiality is key to its existence and the lived experiences of its residents.

ABSOLUTE AND RELATIVE POVERTY

Any attempt to discuss poverty in relation to materiality must begin by exploring what poverty is and who "the poor" actually are. In the simplest sense, poverty is generally considered to be a lack of various kinds of material resources or services, and "the poor" refers to a group of people who fall below a particular minimum standard of wages or living conditions. Yet despite a plethora of official ways of measuring poverty, developed by prominent global organizations such as the United Nations, there is little consensus on how to decide who is poor and who is not. This is because poverty and wealth cannot simply be measured by how much one earns, what kind of household appliances one owns, or even access to clean drinking water. Rather, as social scientists have long argued, poverty and wealth depend on both things and values: the array of material possessions and resources that are at an individual's or family's disposal, and how those material items are incorporated into a system of social values. That is to say, poverty is fundamentally a social arrangement, but it is very much objectified in material form.

If poverty were primarily a lack of material possessions, then hunters and gatherers would be among the poorest people in the world. With no fixed abode and few possessions, all of which they must carry on their backs, their way of living is a far cry from what most people today consider to be a minimum standard. In a world where surveys measure success by income and personal possessions, and even residents of squatter settlements have mobile phones and television sets, hunters and gatherers seem to literally live in the Stone Age. Yet the anthropologist Marshall Sahlins argues that hunters and gatherers are not poor. In his 1972 book *Stone Age Economics*, he calls hunters and gatherers "the original affluent society" because they spend little time working, and they have everything that they need and want. In fact, accumulation of possessions works against them. Because they have to carry everything they own with them when they shift camp, extra items are a burden. While Sahlins's methods have since been criticized for downplaying the amount of contact that his researchers had with sedentary societies, thus possibly misrepresenting their lack of desire for modern things, he does have a very good point: the relationship between poverty and possessions is not straightforward at all.

Mary Douglas and Baron Isherwood make a similar point in their book *The World of Goods: Towards an Anthropology of Consumption* (1978). They use the example of a tribesman with a wealth of livestock but no electricity or air transport, commenting, "What of it? In the universe that he knows, if he has access to all the needful information and can disseminate his own views, he is not poor. The rightful measure of poverty, on this argument, is not possessions, but social involvement" (ibid., 11). More recently, Amartya Sen (1999) has made the point that there are people living in wealthy countries who have fairly high incomes but who are much worse off than low-income-earning people in developing countries, because they do not have access to health care. Thus, we have two extremes that defy our common assumptions about poverty: we have hunters and gatherers who have everything they want, and people living in wealthy countries with a plethora of possessions but who cannot afford the basic necessities of life. Neither are considered well off by today's standards—but then, how do we decide who is poor, especially if they do not see themselves that way?

One problem with Sahlins's study is that it pays little attention to how the lives of the hunters and gatherers he studied were already being negatively affected by the world around them. Throughout the developing world, hunter-and-gatherer populations have frequently been pushed off their land, leaving them with nowhere to go but the planet's slums, marginalized to the edge of cities and struggling to make ends meet (see Davis 2006). Previously they were able to feed themselves through hunting and gathering or peasant agriculture, and organize their own rewarding social and cultural lives. In cities, they are dependent on broader socioeconomic forces and sheer luck in order to survive. Furthermore, they experience a situation of deprivation that they had not faced before: they see other people receiving the benefits of modern life, to which they have little access.

People who have been displaced to slums are not only relatively poor, they also struggle to adjust to a completely new social situation in which well-being and fortunes are tied to a much larger social group. As societies around the world link up, we create our social identities relative to those around us. Yet global society is highly diverse, so creating a social identity is not straightforward. We are faced with what Daniel Miller (1994) calls the "burden of self-creation," meaning that we have more power than ever before to create our own identities and rewarding lives, but we are daunted by the magnitude of the task. Given the vast range of norms, values, and options that exist today, it is difficult to judge how we are faring in comparison to other people. Am I wealthy, or am I poor? What social class do I belong to? Not everyone will answer these questions with the same set of criteria. This is one reason why the answers that barrio residents gave me about their perceptions of their own wealth or poverty were often surprising. They variably described themselves as "poor" or "middle class" depending on who they were comparing themselves to at the time, and what factors they were taking into account.

However, there are nevertheless circumstances in which poverty can, in a practical sense, be said to have an absolute form. Absolute poverty can be defined as a lack of secure access to the basic necessities of life: sufficient nutrition, water, health care, shelter, and possibly also education. Of course, this definition also depends on making value judgments about what *sufficient* means, and so even absolute poverty cannot be completely free from relativity. Nevertheless, I feel that it is useful to have a concept of absolute poverty in order to identify people who face a high risk of incapacitation or death due to lack of access to the basic necessities. Using this measure, we could argue that Sahlins's hunter and gatherers really *were* poor, because their life spans were so much lower than the global standard at the time. Similarly, people who have a high consumption capacity but who cannot afford much-needed health care may also be described as suffering from absolute poverty. Clearly it does not make sense to say that anyone who is dying of an illness is poor—if there is no treatment available to cure them, their predicament is not a matter of wealth or poverty. But in situations where assistance is widely available, but cannot be accessed for lack of money or entitlement, then people can be said to be poor. Thus, absolute poverty includes a notion of unequal distribution or fairness.

There is also the question of whether quantitative measures of poverty accurately identify the poorest sectors of a society. The international poverty line, as measured and used by organizations like the World Bank and the United Nations, attempts to put a universal price on the cost of living. According to their figures, in 2005 there were 1.4 billion people living below the international poverty line, set at US$1.25 per day. National poverty lines tend to differ markedly from country to country and represent a wide range of buying power. For example, in India, the *Socio-Economic and Caste Census 2011* excludes people from being counted as poor if they own a refrigerator or a landline phone (Ministry of Rural Development 2011). But clearly this is not a very useful measure in wealthy countries, where both wages and purchasing power parity are higher. Having twice as much income is not much use if the cost of living is four times higher. The purpose of these indicators is not so much to describe who is and is not poor, but to identify and target populations that need the most assistance. Poverty lines are tools to identify and respond to trends, not universally applicable descriptors of well-being.

So, there is a need for at least two major ways to measure poverty, both of which have objective and subjective aspects. First, there are quantitative tools used for governance, which are used to draw an overall picture of trends, develop policy, and manage delivery of services. These use empirical evidence to make models and calculations, but the indicators that they generate are (by necessity) based on assumptions and generalizations. Second, we can produce qualitative data on poverty to generate "thick descriptions" (Geertz 1973) of who the poor are and how they live. This information can help us refine our models and policies, test our assumptions, and dwell on the more philosophical project of what constitutes a fair and just society, and how we might achieve it. Integral to our understanding of poverty and justice are considerations of what constitutes a reasonable state of material existence in today's global age. To do this, we require an understanding of why material culture matters in the first place.

MORE THAN POVERTY: SELF-CREATION THROUGH MATERIAL CULTURE

Anthropologists have long studied pre-modern objects, such as pots, jewelry, and masks. Over the last few decades, there has been an explosion of research about objects of everyday consumption. The trade of shell necklaces in the Trobriand Islands (Malinowski 1922; Weiner 1992), objects used to convey class distinction in France (Bourdieu 1970), and Aboriginal art (Myers 2002) are now complemented by studies of mobile phones in Jamaica (Horst and Miller 2006), religious paraphernalia in South America (Vásquez 2011), and women getting dressed in London (Woodward 2007). The overall message in all these studies is that consumption is not a shallow and hedonistic activity that humans engage in because modern society has corrupted our values, nor is it simply a means of one-upmanship (of the "my car is better than yours" variety). Rather, consumption, like production, is a process by which we embed values and meanings into things. Just as in pre-modern societies, we use consumption to express our humanity and our beliefs. We give gifts to acknowledge our social relationships and we buy things for ourselves to carve out places of belonging in a dynamic modern world. Modernity—described by Marshall Berman (1982) as including global-historical processes of industrial production, new forms of nation-states, scientific discoveries, and mass communication—has resulted in the democratization of consumption, in the sense that so many products are now available to so many people. The idea that even poor households own televisions and refrigerators is no longer very surprising to many people. In fact, the notion that poor people may even be cosmopolitan in their engagement with consumer culture is also gaining recognition (Thompson 2012).

The problem with viewing consumption as beneficial to humanity is that the ability to consume is unevenly distributed among humankind. Modernity has brought with it new ways of monopolizing global resources and bestowing social status. Furthermore, one could argue that suffering and inequality are not merely unwelcome outcomes of modernity, but were actually integral to the development of modernity itself. Trouillot (1995), among others, has posited that the industrial revolution was funded by slavery in the Americas. Interestingly, Mintz and Price argue that slaves in the Americas played a crucial role in setting the wheels of modernity in motion, and as a result were made into modern subjects before most Europeans, saying, "Long before the common features of the industrial West (imported foods, time-conscious work regimes, factory production, impersonal work relations, etc.) had spread through much of Europe, they were commonplace aspects of life for Caribbean slaves" (Mintz and Price 1985, 9).

The drive to increase sugar production in the Americas propelled the development of new technologies and techniques to manage workers in factories. Whereas most Europeans were still living as peasants, the industrial revolution had already arrived in the Americas. However, slaves were property, not wage laborers, and slave owners used racism to justify their enslavement. Although they were modern subjects, they were not permitted to reap the benefits of modernity. The abolition of slavery permitted at least the hope of access to modernity's possibilities, as it could be put to use to construct new societies and elaborate cultures. Yet the extent to which Caribbean societies were able to break with the stratifications of the past, and the global order that produced them, remains questionable. To this day, the descendants of Africans are disproportionately poor relative to the societies in which they live.

Daniel Miller's (1994) work on material culture in Trinidad presents some interesting insights into the problems of modernity and self-creation. He suggests that a focus on consumption in modern life reveals the strengths of modernity and capitalism: that they generate much wider choices (the "burden of self-creation" that I described above) and possibilities for objectification—using material things to express our social identities. For Miller, our humanity is defined not so much by what we do for a living (our productive roles), but on the things we consume. Whereas Karl Marx considered that we modern humans are alienated from mass-produced goods because we do not make them ourselves, Miller argues that alienation comes from the experience of living in modernity. The problem with modern life is that it presents us with a paradox: we have so many choices available, yet these choices can be overwhelming, causing us to seek social stability as a counterbalance. In other words, modernity bestows in us competing drives to behave conservatively and put down roots, versus making the most of what the world has to offer.

However, alienation does not *have* to result from the condition of modernity. Since rapid change limits people's ability to depend on social relations in shaping their identities, we shift our attempts to create security and stability onto objects. Our homes, mementos, and style of dress can all help give us a sense of having a fixed identity and place in the world. Through such objectifications we realize ourselves as individuals and as social beings and thereby escape alienation. Of course, people who have access to a greater range of goods have more ability to choose the ones that suit their identities. However, Miller argues that this does not mean that objectification is any less important for the poor. Mass-produced goods, rather than being symbols of oppression (through their production by minimum-wage earners) or inequality (through their unequal distribution), hold potential for greater freedoms for humanity around the globe.

MATERIALIZING PRODUCTION: GLOBAL SOCIALITY

While the availability of mass-produced goods increases our options—even for the poor—they are also implicated in the reproduction of poverty. Poor people do not merely lack commodities; they live in stigmatized communities in particular parts of cities and are often also denoted as low status due to their physical appearance. The clothes we wear, the transport we take, and the communities we live in are all part of our "cultural capital" (Bourdieu 1986) that communicates our social status. Importantly, it's not just *what* we own that matters: how we use the things we own is critical to conveying our social identities. For example, I may turn up to a job interview in an expensive new suit, but if I wear, say, a Hawaiian shirt underneath it, I mark myself out as a novice, someone who does not know how to operate properly in the office environment. Similarly, if I can afford to pay for a dinner in an upmarket restaurant, but do not know the norms of table manners, then my companions may be left with the impression that I am pretending to belong to a social class that is higher than the one in which I was brought up. Bourdieu (1984) refers to this need for the right kinds of behaviors as the "habitus," because class-related behaviors become so ingrained in us from the time we are children that we barely notice that they are not innate. Our relationship with material culture, then, is not just something that we can pick and choose: we are socialized into a material world from birth. This places a severe limit on our ability to use modernity's freedoms to our advantage. Certainly we have the ability to shape our own identities, but it can be difficult to completely shed ourselves of one social world in favor of another.

For this reason, the question of identity must look beyond consumption, to how we are produced as social beings by the society in which we are embedded. There is a good reason why one's professional occupation is so often used a measure of social class: what we do as producers—whether factory workers, bankers, teachers, or domestic servants—shapes our ability to consume material resources and the manner in which we consume them. In fact, Donald Robotham (2005) argues that it is not true that our identities are now primarily shaped by consumption; rather, our occupations are still more fundamental to our identities and experiences of modern life. Thousands of years ago, the division of labor allowed small-scale societies to develop specialized craftspeople, such as candlemakers, blacksmiths, bakers, and butchers, making more products available for consumption. Robotham points out that this division of labor now encompasses the entire globe and is the reason why mass consumption exists. Our participation in this global network of production is our most salient experience of modernity and our primary source of identity, because specialization provides a source of social differentiation. Robotham uses the term *global sociality* to describe how the world's people are connected through production, and argues that production links people together more tightly than ever before. It is this global sociality, then, that is the basis of the individual's experience of modern life.

The problem with a global sociality based in production is that while it lays the foundation for a new individuality (where we can choose our own specialized career), it is also the basis of the socioeconomic stratification. Rather than being available to everyone, some groups of people are better able to reap the benefits of the radical division of labor more than others. Growing up in Australia, it did not matter that my family was not wealthy by local standards: I could easily access the resources I needed to attain an excellent education that would be recognized and valued in the workplace. Growing up in Santo Domingo is not so easy: a degree from a public university does not guarantee a job by any means, because competition is fierce and material indicators of social status (including clothing and racial appearance) can trump competence.

However, the handicaps wrought through accidents of birth are not always clearly visible. Diane Austin (1984) describes how, in Jamaica, people come to view their social position as "inherited" and part of the natural social order, rather than due to the workings of massive inequalities in education, racial discrimination, and Jamaica's subordinate position in the global economy. Donald Robotham argues that a major problem is that the market, in appearing to provide opportunity and choice, actually obscures the fact that it is the source of inequalities. The market reduces all forms of value to a common currency that can be consumed through the creation of "identity." In their edited book *Millennial Capitalism*, Jean and John Comaroff discuss the explanation of material differences in terms of identity. They argue, "As neoliberal conditions render ever more obscure the rooting of inequality in structures of production, as work gives way to the mechanical solidarities of 'identity' in constructing selfhood and social being, class comes to be understood, in both popular and scholarly discourse, as yet another personal trait or lifestyle choice" (Comaroff and Comaroff 2001, 15).

Hence Diane Austin-Broos's Jamaicans appear to choose their class position by presenting it as internally generated rather than as the persistence of inequalities that began with plantation slavery. Racial identity is also subject to similar forces. Dark-skinned Dominicans are scapegoated by the national media and by the general public as criminals, who choose to live from easy pickings rather than working hard in a respectable occupation. What we witness here is a process by which one's status as a producer and consumer combine to create imaginary social beings. A "criminal" is judged for his choice of occupation, but how is he identified as a criminal? By the color of his skin, the clothes he wears, and where he lives. Hence, if we want to understand the constraints that people face in their choices, we need to understand how people's capacities as producers and consumers intermix to render them as social beings. Bourdieu's (1986) division of capital into three kinds (economic, social, and cultural) is also helpful here, because some kinds of capital mitigate the effects of others. In some circumstances, the right behaviors (cultural capital) can cancel out the ill effects of having very little money (economic capital). Similarly, the right connections (social capital) could land a publicly educated Dominican (cultural capital) a job with a good income (economic capital). In attempting to describe how poverty works, it is simply impossible to separate production and consumption.

By locating the source of modern individuality in the global division of labor, Robotham allows for individual self-creation, such as through consumption, while recognizing the basis on which it rests. For the individual to flourish under neoliberalism, the sources of inequality must be unmasked. This requires not so much appropriation of objects, but more importantly control of the "determining social forces" that create them (Robotham 2005, 88). Robotham argues that unless the bases for structural inequalities, located in the sphere of production, are appropriated, self-creation will continue to be constrained by one's position in the global division of labor.

One crucial point noted by archaeologists of poverty is that identifying how poverty is created entails looking at the past as well as the present. In the introduction to a special issue of *Historical Archaeology*, Richard (2011) describes how archaeologists are increasingly looking at the material remains of poor settlements to gain insights into how "the poor" actually lived in the past, rather than simply assuming that poverty was a widespread and homogeneous condition. He notes that, far from there being a paucity of possessions to examine in poor communities, "the city poor nevertheless purchased and discarded a great variety of material culture and participated actively, though perhaps unevenly, in spheres of urban consumption" (2011, 174). Hence by tapping into both poverty as lived experience and the structural conditions that shape it, accounts of poverty's materiality can "combine an appreciation for the poor's condition of life, coping strategies, and tactics of resistance, with an acknowledgment of the extreme inequality churning up the raw material out of which subaltern ways of belonging and being in the world are crafted" (Richard 2011, 170). Poverty is not an eternal condition: as difficult as it may be to escape it, the experience of poverty—and our definitions of what poverty is—change over time. Hence, while examining an individual's experiences of oppression or freedom can tell us a great deal about how poverty is lived, we must examine society at large to understand how poverty is produced.

MORE THAN ARTIFACTS: OBJECTS, BODIES, AND SPACES

All this discussion of production and consumption makes one thing particularly clear: when we talk about the role that the material world plays in stratification, we are not just talking about objects that can be bought and sold. The physical appearance of people and places is just as strongly implicated in status judgments and experiences of poverty and wealth. In other words, material culture consists of more than human-made objects: it includes the properties of different kinds of material things and their collective contribution to the social, cultural, and economic lives of human beings. In order to understand how materiality shapes the agency of individuals, it can be helpful to examine materiality in terms of three properties: control over property and resources (economy), control over sociocultural meanings (semiotics), and the properties of the material forms themselves (aesthetics). These properties can be intrinsic to the thing itself (its aesthetics, such as color and shape), or bestowed externally (its social meaning). They can have economic value (a pair of earrings costs five dollars) and symbolic value (the style of the earrings indicates the gender of the wearer). This kind of analysis is useful to understanding any social situation, but is particularly useful for understanding poverty in multiple dimensions.

For example, a squatter settlement takes its appearance (aesthetic) from the materials that its builder had at hand, such as sheets of plywood and corrugated iron, because the builder cannot afford to buy many materials (economic). These kinds of found materials are of much lower quality and status than regular building materials such as factory-cut timber, bricks, and steel. Not only is the house inferior from a practical point of view, but it also offers insufficient protection against the weather and signifies low status. Economically, the house has little value; symbolically, it has low status, and aesthetically, it falls short of cultural norms. But this individual house is not judged in isolation. Entire urban suburbs are viewed as low status due to their material appearance. The people who live there are also deemed to be of low status, and possibly also immoral. To distinguish themselves from the poor masses, the wealthier classes consume a different style of objects than the poor do (Bourdieu 1984). Physical appearance, including skin color, hair color, hairstyle, and weight, forms part of class-specific norms that contribute to social differentiation. So, if we want to understand the role of materiality in poverty —which is significant—then we also need to understand how bodies and spaces are implicated in this process, how they are given meaning and value by their producers and consumers, and how they are judged by observers.

The first step is to look at how different objects work together to create meaning. As Douglas and Isherwood (1978) point out, objects can generally only be understood in relation to one another. The example they use is of the decoration of a lounge room. The amount of ornamentation used, the care with which it is implemented, the kinds of objects present, and the value of those objects are all intrinsic to understanding the motives of the person who decorated the room and their place in society. The presence of a couple of ornaments will probably not tell you what their significance is to their owner; they might be prized possessions, or they might be afterthoughts. It is highly likely that the designer's explanation will not just deal with those ornaments, but also reveal the logic of their placement in the room relative to other objects (their proxemics). Similarly, a single book will not tell you much about the preferences of the reader, but a library speaks volumes. The absence of personal possessions can also tell you a lot about a person. Miller's description in *The Comfort of Things* (2008) of a man whose London house is almost threadbare is the most striking example of this that I have ever come across: he has no things, because he has no social life to represent.

The trick with a material analysis that takes proxemics into account is that it is concerned not only with why objects are placed in one collection, but also with their distribution in space (e.g., minimalist or cluttered) and their relation to the human body (e.g., personal or shared possessions). This appears to pose a definitional problem. Material culture is generally thought of as the use of artifacts made by human beings, excluding natural objects (Prown 1982). Things become material culture as soon as they are perceived by human beings, because whenever we sense an object we classify it according to our cultural categories. The human body and the landscape have an independent physical existence that does not depend on human culture, yet they are incorporated into material culture just as readily as any other object. We assign them with value judgments and meanings that are products of the human imagination. Furthermore, the human body and the landscape affect how we manipulate objects. A chair's ergonomics conform to the shape of the human body; a beach umbrella is adapted to the properties of sand. As Pierre Bourdieu's (1970) famous study of the Berber house clearly demonstrates, we design our houses to fit in with our own bodies and the landscape. Nancy Munn (1996) has argued that the creation of culturally meaningful spaces depends on the movement of a social group through space, and so it is not possible to talk about a landscape without recognizing that it is viewed through the senses of people.

One important point to note is how *materiality* is transformed into *material culture.* The landscape and the human body, though clearly possessing materiality, are not immediately classifiable as material culture if they have not been given social and cultural meanings. However, it is arguable that there is no material thing that can be witnessed by human beings and not interpreted according to our ways of seeing the world. All material things, then, become culturally constructed as soon as they are perceived by human beings. They are, as Harré defines it, "social substances," which are "material stuff that belongs to a category that is defined in terms of the properties of some social world" (2002, 24). Thus, alcohol is not necessarily a social substance, because it is a generic category that is found in a variety of sites including bars and laboratories. However, communion wine is a social substance because it has one specific use. His definition is useful because it recognizes that making material forms meaningful is a process that can be realized cognitively as well as physically.

In fact, although Harré indicates the transformation of a thing from a category to a social substance by presenting a shift in its name (from alcohol to communal wine), this linguistic shift is not necessary. Though common, not all material things are renamed once we shift our thinking from viewing them as a generic item to a thing with a specific social use. For example, Sahlins (1991) shows how some animals are renamed for human consumption (a "cow" is a living animal, but when it is on our supermarket shelves we call it "beef") while others are not (a "duck" is both a living animal and a product for our consumption). Even geographical features sometimes struggle to lose their association with their original name. As I shall discuss later, a swamp is a natural feature of a landscape, but the word can also be used to indicate that a place is uninhabitable. When Dominicans settled in **la ciénaga** (the swamp), it officially became a neighborhood called La Ciénaga (The Swamp). That is, the addition of people transformed the site from a natural substance into a social substance. The social meanings of the barrio are constituted by a material culture that extends far beyond the consumption practices of its residents.

THE MATERIALITY OF SQUATTING: INTRODUCING LA CIÉNAGA

The visitor arriving at Santo Domingo's international airport enjoys a pleasant taxi ride into the capital city along the well-maintained Las Americas expressway that runs parallel to the calm, blue Caribbean Sea. Along the way, monuments and sculptures promote the nation as a cultural destination, while billboards advertise locally popular products: Maggi stock, Presidente beer, and Brugal rum. Dusty lots of three-story, pastel-colored, concrete-rendered apartments sit separated from the sea by the bustle of cars, minibuses, and motorbikes.

The heart of the city lies on the far side of the Ozama River. Most tourists are introduced into the national district via the floating bridge that leads straight to the *zona colonial* (colonial zone), which is the old Spanish city and the capital's main tourist destination. The majority of traffic, however, enters the city via the twin Duarte and Bosch bridges (figure 1.1). Looking left from these bridges, one sees the colonial zone with its fine Spanish architecture, shops selling cigars and postcards, and restaurants offering international cuisine. Located where the Caribbean Sea meets the Ozama River, and boasting kilometers of paved waterfront, it is the center of Santo Domingo's social life with plenty of places for tourists and locals alike to enjoy a cold beer.

Looking right, one sees thousands of tiny tin-roofed houses packed in close together, partially hidden by tropical greenery. Built right up to the water's edge, they seem as though they are poised to slip into the river. This is La Ciénaga. Because the main entry into La Ciénaga is located directly underneath the twin bridges, the barrio is referred to as *abajo el puente* [sic], meaning "under the bridge." It is arguably the most infamous of Santo Domingo's squatter settlements, renowned nationwide for its poverty, clearly visible to anyone crossing the twin bridges. Indeed, the historian Jesse Hoffnung-Garskof notes that "be-

Figure 1.1.   The twin bridges spanning the Ozama River, seen from La Ciénaga.
Photograph courtesy of the author.

cause it was visible to anyone crossing the Juan Bosch bridge, La Ciénaga became emblematic to Santo Domingo residents who commonly
referred to any marginal settlement as 'under the bridge'" (Hoffnung-
Garskof 2008, 41). To live under the bridge is to live precariously, no
matter where one is physically located.

La Ciénaga is one of the poorest of Santo Domingo's barrios. It is
located just a few kilometers from the center of Santo Domingo, but it
was not settled until after the death of the dictator Rafael Trujillo in
1961. Before settlement, the area was used as farmland by working-
class families living nearby. They cultivated rice, coconuts, and other
crops in its fertile, flood-prone soil. Since the 1960s, migrants have
transformed the swamp into an urban community. Many of the original
settlers who arrived in the 1960s and 1970s came from the fertile Cibao
valley (which includes the ex-capital city of Santiago), traditionally considered to be the heartland of Dominican national identity (Martínez-
Vergne 2005).

Fay and Wellenstein state that 11 percent of Santo Domingo's population (approximately 300,000 people) resides in inner-city barrios
around the Ozama River (2005, 97). Although the term *barrio* literally
means "neighborhood," it implies that residents are poor and the area
consists of substandard housing. The term *barrio* **pobre** (poor neighborhood) is often used for emphasis. Santo Domingo's barrios are overwhelmingly populated by migrants from rural areas. Approximately 60
percent of residents originated from the arid southwest of the country,
22 percent from the agricultural center of Cibao, and just 5 percent
from the southeast, the country's largest tourist region (Tejeda 2000,
33). Rural migrants have built communities around the river, drawing
on networks of friends and relatives in the city to find housing and
employment. Rural Dominicans migrate to cities primarily because of a
changing economic balance between the countryside and the city that
leaves them few options in the countryside. Economic opportunities in
the country have diminished severely over the past century as large
companies have acquired peasant landholdings and population has out-
stripped supply of arable land for peasant production (Dore y Cabral
1981). At the same time, urban centers have industrialized, creating
jobs in manufacturing and services.

According to the surveys I conducted in 2005 and 2009, the majority
of employed persons in La Ciénaga work in the city's informal sector.
Women primarily work as domestic servants in the homes of the middle
class, or sell products (e.g., homemade juice or ice cream, beauty products, or nonperishable goods) from their homes. Men work as ambulatory vendors in the city, take passengers on their motorbikes from La
Ciénaga to the top of the cliff, labor in the construction industry, manage grocery stores within the barrio, or work as security guards for
apartment blocks and city offices. There are, of course, exceptions.
Alternative professions include engineers, lawyers, secretaries, teachers, computer technicians, and nuns, but on the whole, *cienigüeros*
(residents of La Ciénaga) find that the range of occupations available to
them is limited. My surveys suggest that the average full-time salary is
around 8,000–10,000 pesos per month (US$195–245), and the highest
salary that was reported to me in 2009 was 20,000 pesos per month
(US$488), earned by a grocery store owner, a lawyer, and a doctor.
However, wages vary widely, especially for men who work in *chiripero*
(doing odd jobs). While collecting data on income is difficult due to

fluctuations and reporting bias, I estimate that the average yearly salary is around US$2,500.

Turning into La Ciénaga's sole entrance, there is a pretty street lined with newly planted trees and designs painted onto the bridge's columns. This entrance was renovated by the municipal council in 2010. The Ozama River runs alongside to the right, barricaded off by brightly colored railings. The visitor passes the new fire station, the military post, the salami factory, a basketball court, and numerous people buying street food and hanging out to the sounds of *bachata* (a Dominican style of music) and motorbikes passing. Turning right will take you to a hill in the center of the barrio (known as **La Clarín**), where the school and church are located. The barrio's entrance and this central region are considered the nicest parts of the barrio, the public face where visitors and passers-by can admire the "progress" that is seeping into the squatter settlements from the city.

The lower part of the barrio, however, presents a major contrast. If you head downhill and duck into the nearest alleyway, the housing soon becomes irregular. Soon the concrete-paved paths run out and one must clamber over rocks and planks to bypass the large dirty puddles left by the summer rain. You will pass over canals full of ***agua negra*** (black water), water so dirty that it looks like it came straight out of an oil well, emitting a substance akin to the miasmatic gas that Engels (1987 [1887]) described in the canals of nineteenth-century Manchester. Kids play in houses that have half-sunk into the swamp. Their owners, hoping to create better living standards, converted them from shacks to concrete block, but they were tragically too heavy to withstand the pull of the mud.

It is here in the lower part of the barrio that you get a sense of why it is called La Ciénaga. Despite decades of filling in the swamp with garbage, and recent improvements to drainage, many of the lower parts of the barrio remain precarious and pose serious health problems for their inhabitants. The contrast between ***abajo*** (lit. "below," meaning the low land in the swamp and around the river's edge) and ***arriba*** (lit. "above," meaning the high land in the center of the barrio and near the barrio's main entrance) is both physically and socially marked, to the extent that it constitutes the barrio's own moral geography that closely resembles the stigma placed on the barrio (figure 1.2).

La Ciénaga is an ideal case study for examining how materiality is enabling for people living in poverty at the same time as it constrains them. Some residents suffer from abject poverty, and all are socially stigmatized by virtue of their material poverty. But living in a squatter settlement, though a poorer environment than neighboring working-class suburbs, facilitates self-creation, sociality, and what the Dominicans call "progress," in ways that would be difficult to achieve outside the barrio. Their successes are by and large the outcome of their everyday actions in developing their social-material relations, and in their persistence with this project over a long period of time. In essence, they live out what Diane Austin-Broos (2009) calls a "standing fight": faced with an ambivalent state, which varies between including them and marginalizing them, they dig in their heels and continue about their everyday lives to the best of their abilities, given the resources they have at hand. This book depicts their struggle.

Figure I.2. Small houses in various stages of construction, located in La Ciénaga's low ground near the Ozama River. *Photograph courtesy of the author.*

2

BUILDING FUTURES

Squatting as an Enabling Constraint

It was a normal day at Adela's house. She had just fed her neighbor's children la bandera *(the flag), a lunch of beans, rice, and chicken that is named after the Dominican flag, and sent them off to school, when Maria dropped in for their daily exchange of food. Maria, being fonder of cooking than Adela, had prepared flour dumplings, fried eggplant, and rice. Every day, each woman exchanges a bowlful of lunch so that their families have a greater variety to eat. It is also an excuse to exchange information and greetings.*

That day, Maria and Adela were concerned about Maria's thirty-one-year-old son (also Adela's second cousin) Marco, who had not had regular employment for three years. Adela was interested in his current plans, and asked Maria, "So, Marco says he's going to join the fire brigade?"

Maria responded, "He says so, and he's found out how to go about it, but the trial period is five months."

"Five months?" exclaimed Adela, "Oh that's long. Well, he has to do something. I told him so. Last I heard he was going to move to Puerto Plata."

"He changed his mind because he didn't have anywhere to stay there, not a bed or anything," explained Maria, pausing at the door.

"I told him that he needs to do something so that he can have children. I said, 'You can't grow old without having had children. They're

the ones who care for you. If not, you have nothing.' He needs to build
his house."

This conversation, which took place in 2005, illustrates lucidly the relationship between material and social reproduction. The need to have a
stable income in order to build a house and have a family is a problem
for poor men and women alike. More than any other material object,
the house nurtures the family by providing stability and protection.
Since "family reproductive strategies are both constrained and facilitated by house durability and fixity to site" (Birdwell-Pheasant and Lawrence-Zuñiga 1999, 27), Marco must embed himself successfully within
relations of economic reproduction and convert them into material
form in order to reproduce himself socially.

In this chapter I use the term *enabling constraint* to describe how
the things that limit people in life can also be some of their most useful
tools and resources to get ahead. In La Ciénaga, the self-built home is
very much one of these objects that brings benefits as much as limitations. On the one hand, investing years into the construction of a home
locks one into place: when the sum total of a family's capital is literally
cemented into the ground, there is little freedom to take up new directions should the opportunity or desire arise. But on the other hand,
home ownership under these conditions provides its own freedoms—
economic and social—which are highly valuable. They include not having to pay rent, the greater facility for family members to live near each
other, and pride in being able to build and decorate a home. These are
not just convenient side effects; they are the reasons why people choose
to live in areas that are generally highly stigmatized, and sometimes
physically dangerous.

I extend the concept of "creativity within constraint" to argue that
residents of Santo Domingo's barrios are not simply doing the best they
can within the constraints that face them. Rather, they are actively
using those constraints to their own advantage to achieve things that
would otherwise be difficult, if not impossible. Constructing one's own
home on a tight budget and in a poor community marks out the homeowners as low status, thus constraining their socioeconomic mobility.
However, autoconstruction and illegality enables residents to gather
family members around them, building a social support network that is
objectified in the barrio's streets and houses. It also provides freedom

from having to pay rent, more living space, and greater security of residence. I contend that it is incorrect to view autoconstruction as a zero-sum game in which residents achieve little but reproduce the conditions of their marginalization or perhaps extend a mild form of "resistance" to the state. Autoconstruction is not merely a "choice of the necessary" (Bourdieu 1984), something that poor people do because they literally have no other options. The physical autoconstruction of the built environment is central to the struggle for self-creation and autonomy for residents of Santo Domingo's squatter settlements. Interestingly, the process of bypassing state regulations has permitted residents to create a neighborhood that increasingly resembles a Dominican ideal of an urban community. As I will describe in chapter 3, cienigüeros, through striking out on their own, have actually attached themselves to the state by campaigning for social goods including official recognition, schools, health services, political representation, electricity, transport, and incorporation into official urban planning.

This chapter begins by explaining the term *enabling constraint* and introducing my case study. I then present three ways that the constraints of autoconstruction enable creativity and provide tangible benefits. First, an initial lack of state investment in the barrio meant that residents had to design and build the streets they live in as well as their homes. This was a time-consuming and costly exercise that compelled residents to live in unsatisfactory conditions for years. However, by constructing the barrio themselves, residents determined how people would socialize within it, which brought significant advantages. Second, there is no enforcement of building regulations, which is problematic from a safety point of view but permits residents to construct their houses in their own time and change their plans as they see fit. Third, residents have very little money with which to properly finish and furnish the house according to the Dominican norms of what a modern house should look like: made of concrete, with tiled floors and white metal shutters on the windows. While an unfinished house and its not-quite-right furnishings are both markers of poverty and an ongoing source of frustration, residents often express the opinion that their perseverance with this task, despite the difficulties they face, is evidence of their own morality. In contrast, people who do not invest in home improvement are considered morally suspect. Hence the incompleteness of squatter settlements cannot merely be viewed as a losing battle against poverty. Rather, squatter settlements are testimony to the creativity and aspirations of their inhabitants in the face of difficult circumstances.

THE ENABLING PROPERTIES OF AUTOCONSTRUCTION

To what extent can marginalized people truly have agency? This question has been debated extensively in studies of Caribbean societies. The concept of "creativity within constraint" has been used to acknowledge that it is inaccurate to describe the region's peoples solely in terms of domination. Rex Nettleford (1971) and others argue rightly that enslaved Africans exhibited an astonishing degree of creativity in their efforts to build an entirely new society and culture. Their cultural production was impressive and testimony to the capacities of human beings for collaborative creativity under the worst kinds of duress.

Diane Austin (1983) theorized the concept more thoroughly, using the phrase *conflict contained by domination* in her observations that scholars of the English-speaking Caribbean tend to view those societies either in terms of opposition (the masses resist the dominant powers) or domination (resistance is impossible). She posited instead that the working classes were indeed producing oppositional culture, their own institutions, and even their own ideologies, but their efforts were ultimately constrained because they could not escape from ideological domination by the ruling classes.

What I would like to suggest is that the constraints observed in both these cases are very real, and place hard limits on choice, but that the effects of the constraints themselves deserve a second look. Constraints do not necessarily make all action grind to a halt; rather, they can create barriers in certain directions, but they can also provide new opportunities. The term *enabling constraint* has its roots in the work of the seventeenth-century liberal political theorists Thomas Hobbes and John Locke, who observed that sovereign authorities impose limits on their citizens, but they also free us from many of the constraints that other individuals might impose on us. For example, I am compelled to stop my car at a red light, which limits my agency, but it also permits me to drive far more safely than would be possible without rules. The concept has since been taken up by information theory, biology, and social psychology, among others. It also holds true for society and culture: we create our collective lives out of the resources we have at hand, and if those resources are limited, we invent novel ways to achieve our goals, which can have positive side effects.

Of course, there is no guarantee that the positive outcomes will outweigh the negative ones. In places where abject poverty is endemic, the enabling properties of constraints are unlikely to address the structural causes of poverty. Even when people achieve socioeconomic mobility—which is often—they are likely to climb slowly through the system without significantly altering the mechanisms by which socioeconomic stratification is reproduced. However, recognizing that positive outcomes can be achieved challenges our assumptions that poor communities and the people who live in them are lost causes. Rather than viewing the poor as trapped in a "cycle of poverty," scholars have developed tools to recognize the significant limitations that the poor face without viewing those limitations as insurmountable. For example, Paul Farmer's analysis of "structural violence" in Haiti (1997; 2004) and Kleinman, Das, and Lock's use of the term *social suffering* (1997) are just two examples of the contributions that social scientists have made to our understandings of the bases of inequality and how it is experienced. There is an enormous body of work on the concept of hegemony that details how power is symbolically reproduced. Yet the things that marginalized peoples do to alter their own lives cannot be reduced to resisting hegemony. Many of the gains they make are the result of living out their everyday lives, in a fashion that suits them, with little consideration of the political implications of their actions. Poor people improve their lives by doing things they enjoy, as well as struggling against adversity.

The anthropologist James Holston (1991) recognizes this dynamic very well. Writing about the construction of favelas in Brazil, he uses the term *autoconstruction* to describe owner-builders in illegal settlements. He avoids the term *squatting* because it implies illegality, as in Brazil especially, squatter settlements are often formalized. Even in La Ciénaga, where residents do not have land title, it is not clear whether they are really illegal: they often own documents showing ownership for their houses, and there is no legal consensus on who actually owns the land they occupy. Holston describes how Brazilian state policy shifted in the 1980s from viewing squatter settlements as a social problem that needed to be removed, to legalizing settlements and providing them with services in the hope of attaining social stability and a domesticated labor market. Holston views this shift in policy ambiguously, arguing that while autoconstruction benefits the poor, it also reinforces their subordinate position. On the one hand, autoconstruction challenges the subjugation of the poor, "replacing these [negative] images with new ones of competence and knowledge in the production and consumption of [modern goods]" (Holston 1991, 462). On the other hand, "the working class are grounding themselves in a spatialized industrialism in which their position at the bottom of the socioeconomic hierarchy is inscribed upon space and reinforced" (Holston 1991, 450). Holston argues that "the paradox of autoconstruction is that it develops through the reiteration of the kinds of property relations that ground the very social order that exploits them as workers. Although this reproduction changes what is reproduced, I argue that it also expands it scope and power by inscribing it in new places" (1991, 448).

In simple terms, Holston is arguing that constructing working-class suburbs is part of what keeps people working class. We could paint a similar picture for Santo Domingo's autoconstructed settlements. They are a desirable place for new immigrants from the countryside to settle, because they provide access to both land and employment opportunities. An ongoing court battle between the state and a wealthy family over legal ownership has kept the land off the market, allowing poor migrants to obtain plots at a minimal cost (see chapter 3). However, autoconstruction is a risky long-term strategy because it requires the investment of all of a household's resources into the house without land security. Residents' investments could easily be lost in the case of a natural disaster or a state eviction. Living without legal tenure therefore imposes a double alienation from socioeconomic life, as residents are insecure and disadvantaged in both the labor market and the property market.

Nevertheless, in my view, the creativity of autoconstruction needs to be given separate voice from the structural conditions that propel it. For this reason I suggest that we think about it as an enabling constraint. It does indeed have the effects identified by Holston (1991) of locking people into place, but it also drastically increases people's ability to look after themselves and their families with increased autonomy and freedom. It enables people to accumulate capital and express themselves aesthetically through the construction and decoration of their homes, and it gives them a remarkably high degree of autonomy within the localities in which they live. Within their communities, squatter settlement residents can exert their control over their built environment to construct meaningful social relationships, both for the purpose of helping each other cope with poverty and as an end in itself. Through autoconstruction, residents increase their control over their social relationships and their own creative self-realizations. They generate an "inalienable culture" (Miller 1987, 17) that they are unlikely to find in their working lives, as domestic servants, construction workers, shop assistants, and street vendors. These freedoms are generally not available to poor, urban residents whose material existence is subject to the will of landlords and the state.

ESTABLISHING A FOOTHOLD

In the early days of settlement, La Ciénaga resembled a rural environment far more than an urban one. Daniel, a local politician who lived in La Ciénaga between 1966 and 1977, remembers playing in the swamp as a teenager:

> In the late 1950s we used to go down to the swamp to catch crabs and sell them in the city. We would bathe in the *agua dulce* [lit. sweet water] of the river and we made a field to play baseball. In 1964 a Puerto Rican engineer filled in the swamp and people started to settle there soon after the 1965 revolution.

Since then, migrants have transformed the farmland into an urban community. After Trujillo's death in 1961, the land around the river was populated by people already residing in Santo Domingo and by new migrants, all of whom were looking for a plot of land where they could build a house. The city allowed access to a larger labor market at a time when agriculture was dwindling, as well as the chance to take advantage of the benefits of modern city living, such as education.

Daniel's brother Cristino was one of the original founders of La Ciénaga. Before he moved his family to La Clarín (the high ground in the center of the barrio named after its landmark radio tower), there was just a handful of wood-and-tin shacks scattered on this high, dry land and at the barrio's entrance. La Ciénaga was not a place for families to live: it was swampland used for growing rice and vegetables by residents of neighboring Guachupita. In fact, before the Dominican dictator Rafael Leónidas Trujillo was assassinated in 1961, anyone who settled in La Ciénaga was forcibly removed by the state. Cristino's arrival in 1972 spearheaded the slow influx of new occupants looking for space to house their young, growing families. It was in this period that La Ciénaga began to take its urban form. Cristino's story is worth telling in full because his life course from country to city is typical of many barrio residents.

Cristino was born in 1925 in Constanza, an agricultural town located in the mountains on the western edge of Cibao. His father was a landed peasant who died when Cristino was around eight years old. The family lost their land to a neighbor, who had fraudulently created a land title covering the property. Cristino was not able to attend school, as he and his elder brother had to work to look after their mother and younger brothers and sisters. He found few opportunities in the countryside, so he moved to Santo Domingo (not far from La Ciénaga) in the late 1940s to work in the construction industry. In 1972, he married his wife, Maria, who is twenty years his junior and also from Cibao. In the same year, Cristino bought a small piece of land on the central, rocky high ground in La Ciénaga. At the time, his elder brother Daniel was already living on the main road, near the entrance to La Ciénaga. There were no roads or services in the area, and residents have clear memories of the difficulties they faced in the 1970s. Cristino's eldest son, Felix, who was one of the first children to be born in La Ciénaga, explained his family's decision:

> We emigrated from the country to the city and the place with the conditions for us to be able to establish ourselves was La Ciénaga, because in contrast to the center of the city, a site so isolated as this wasn't important to anyone. Everyone who came here got land and stayed. It was a difficult life because the streets weren't paved, the system of electricity was even worse than now, and the water almost never arrived as far as our house, perhaps once per week.

Cristino built his own home on high ground in the center of the barrio. When he had constructed a small wooden **ranchito** (house) with a dirt floor, as well as rice fields and vegetable plots in the unused marsh behind his house, he brought his new wife to live with him. As well as growing his own food, Cristino continued to work in construction.

Also in 1972, Cristino convinced his thirty-eight-year-old cousin Adela to buy a plot of land in La Clarín. At that time, Adela was living in Guachupita with her four children in a tiny room that Cristino described as "a *pedacito* [little piece of space] with just enough room for a double bed and no room to move around it." Adela explained her decision to move to La Ciénaga to me:

> Well, I lived in Guachupita and I was working hard washing and ironing clothes. I had a tiny house without enough room to build a toilet and I was **luchando** [struggling]. My cousin Cristino saw my situation and he said to me, "Adela, why don't you buy a block of land there in the *monte* [wilderness] where I bought one, because there one can be tranquil and live well with a lot of space." And I had saved thirty pesos so I said to him, "Well, all right, I'm going to go down there." I went down and bought this little piece of **monte** here. There was already a ranchito but it was in a bad state of repair. I went up a ladder with nails and a hammer, and I finished it myself. I only put on a roof of *cartón negro* [particle board] because I didn't have enough money to buy zinc. So I moved in here and sold my house arriba.

Adela invested fifty pesos (at that time equivalent to US$50) in repairing her ranchito of four walls, a dirt floor, and a tin roof. The house was small, but far more spacious than Adela's rented flat; moreover, there was plenty of room for expansion in the almost-vacant barrio. As a single mother with very limited resources, Adela depended on her work and her reputation as a respectable person to obtain the credit necessary to buy her ranchito. The sale of her small house in Guachupita funded the repairs she made to the house. At that time, the barrio was what Dominicans call *puro monte*: pure wilderness with no electricity, no sealed roads, and just one pipe running water into the barrio. It was difficult to access on foot, let alone by motorized transport. Adela remarked:

> When I arrived in La Ciénaga it was *monte destruído* [destroyed wilderness]. There were very few people here and we couldn't help each other too much because we were all poor. There were few houses or people; the majority of the place was pure monte. We grew

rice in the swamp below and there were crabs everywhere. We woke up eating crab and every second day I would send my son to sell them so that we could buy food.

When it rained you couldn't go up the cliff into the city and we would have to wear gumboots. We all finished building our houses in the rainy season because the military couldn't come here to evict us because there was so much water. But then they installed a drainage system so many people moved here and built houses. This was a river before and now there is little water.

Adela's memories of the early days are of a threatening natural environment that lacked the social life that gives a value to place. Her landscape was populated by scuttling crabs that could be caught and eaten or sold in markets, and she struggled to create a home for herself and her children. Besides growing food with Cristino, Adela took in ironing. Most days she would walk up the muddy path into the city to collect freshly washed clothes from her clients and cart them back to her ranchito. At home she had a wood-burning stove on which she heated her metal iron.

For Adela, life in La Ciénaga was better than her former home in the city only because there was more space for herself and her children and she could be close to her cousin and his family. In all other respects, Adela felt that she was struggling against daunting barriers. Adela's comment that she built her house during the rainy season refers to the fact that there was a presidential decree declaring that the land was to remain uninhabited. Residents could build relatively safely in the rainy season, when the military found it difficult to access the high land of the area. These were the early days of the barrio when there were still very few residents, the streets were unpaved, there was no drainage, and there were no utilities or services.

Adela and Cristino purchased their houses from one of the very few people living in the barrio for prices that they considered to be a bargain. The man who sold them the land did not hold the land title himself, which explains its low cost. At that time, the barrio was virtually empty, so Cristino and Adela grew rice and vegetables in the large tracts of swamp behind their house. Adela made money washing and ironing clothes for middle-class city residents. She would trudge up the dirt path to the top of the cliff every day to collect and return clean, neatly folded clothes—never an easy task in the rainy season when the barrio turned to mud. Cristino gained steady employment in a local government program to restore colonial architecture. He retired in 1990 and receives a monthly pension of 2,000 pesos (around US$60). His wife Maria had to retire from cleaning houses part-time due to health problems, but they also receive support from their sons.

TIME AND SPACE TO GROW

Cristino, Adela, and every other early resident began their residence in La Ciénaga in a ranchito. In their early stages of development, ranchitos have a dirt floor, a roof made of board or tin (possibly waterproofed with tar), walls of boards or tin, no internal ceiling, one or two rooms, and wooden shutters for windows. Internal walls are often lined with reams of material, such as old curtains, and posters or pictures from magazines. A pit latrine and a sheltered bathing area are located in the backyard. If there is a kitchen, it is equipped with a stove fueled by a gas tank. Double beds provide somewhere to sleep for multiple family members, and most clothing is stored in the dresser or between the mattresses.

Crucial to understanding why people would want to build a house in a barrio is the knowledge that not only is there little legal oversight but there is also no time limit on construction so long as residents are not evicted. Over many years, perhaps even generations, residents improve their homes as resources permit, until they eventually conform to aesthetic (if not legal) norms of what a modern urban dwelling should be (figure 2.1). Every ranchito is constructed with the intention that it will eventually be transformed into a house that would meet the standards of respectability anywhere in the city. Throughout the Dominican Republic, a respectable house is made of concrete block with a tiled concrete floor and a concrete slab roof. It has white metal shutters, bars on the windows, and air conditioning in the main bedroom. Residents of the barrios as much as elsewhere in this city aspire to this ideal, although it may take them decades to achieve or be left for the next generation to complete.

There is a standard method to transform one's house, and most barrio streets will include houses at various stages of construction. Once the concrete floor and posts are installed, the walls are filled with con-

Figure 2.1. **This autoconstructed home is a common design in the barrio.** *Photograph courtesy of the author.*

crete blocks. Generally, the front wall is the first to be converted from tin to block, as it is the physical and reputational façade of the family (see also Holston 1991). White metal shutters and bars may also be installed, depending upon the disposition and consumption power of the owner. If the owners of a house come into a sum of money through better employment or the success of a child, they replace the wood-and-tin roof with a concrete plate and rewire internally. A concrete roof serves as both the internal ceiling and the external roof. The house's steel rod and concrete supports are left exposed at the top, so that a second level can be added to the house when the owners accumulate sufficient resources (figure 2.2). The roof of the first floor will then serve as a floor and the second level will be topped with either a tin or concrete-plate roof. A concrete roof is more desirable because it provides better protection against hurricanes and is also a place to hang out the washing. However, houses with plate roofs are hotter inside than those with triangular tin roofs because the air cannot circulate over the internal walls. The design of Adela's house is particularly conducive to catching the cool afternoon breezes that come from the river and sea, because its roof is tin and its front and back doors are aligned to aid the circulation of air. Her nephew Diego owns a much "better" two-level concrete house with plate ceilings, but it is insufferable during the summer. Since most people in La Ciénaga are too poor to afford air conditioning, achieving the ideal aesthetic (and a safer dwelling) can actually cause loss of comfort.

Cienigüeros use a wide variety of strategies to obtain the resources necessary to build and transform their house, not all of which are realizable within the barrio itself. While Cristino remained in Santo Domingo all his life, and spent a considerable amount of time restoring colonial buildings for the municipal council, Adela spent eleven years working overseas as a domestic servant, leaving her (by then) grown-up children by themselves. She explains:

Figure 2.2. A three-level concrete block house, divided into apartments, sits next to one of the few remaining ranchitos in La Ciénaga's high ground. *Photograph courtesy of the author.*

In 1978 I went to Venezuela and left my children here in this little wooden house, which was falling apart around them. They were already grown up. It wasn't a large house, just a little ranchito with a dirt floor. I left here and each month sent my earnings to my children so that they could buy food. I was working hard for very little in return. I was always hungry as my employers didn't give me enough to eat. In time my children all got jobs and told me, "Mama, don't send us any more money; we're all working. Save the little money you earn to build a house." After four years I came back to visit and I marked out where the house should go, and when I returned for good after eleven years the house was already done: my children had built it.

Adela's earnings in Venezuela allowed her to transform her ranchito into a **casa buena** (good house) of concrete block with a tin roof. It has two and a half bedrooms and an indoor bathroom that she received for free from a community project to provide sanitation in the barrio. All her windows have metal shutters and the front windows have metal bars. Since the electricity supply was somewhat more regular than when she had left, Adela invested her savings in a refrigerator and a chest freezer, as well as items of furniture. She also has a gas tank for cooking. These purchases allowed Adela to run her own business from home, selling homemade *mabí* (sugary juice), ice cream, and ice from her living room. Adela's income is supplemented by money from one of her daughters who moved to Puerto Rico, as well as assistance from her cousin's family if absolutely necessary. She continues to grow food in her garden, such as passion fruit and bananas. Until a few years ago she had a large tamarind tree whose fruit she would use to make mabí. Adela would climb this tree to pick the fruit or simply to catch the afternoon breeze. She would look for any excuse to climb it, such as to cut off a branch that was blocking the light to her house. Her nephews, worried that she was too old to climb the tree safely, eventually convinced her to let them poison the tree. They were certainly not going to climb it themselves to collect its fruit: as they pointed out, this was a task for people like Adela who had grown up in the country and done this kind of thing their entire lives.

Adela's income is very small and she is sometimes reduced to cooking in the backyard with firewood when she cannot afford gas, but she considers herself to be quite well-off because she owns a spacious, well-located house, has all the possessions she desires, and is surrounded by her family and friends. She is proud that her children will be able to inherit the property one day, and has a funeral fund and savings in the bank so that her passing away will not be a burden on them. Far from seeking extra help, Adela goes out of her way to help others. She generously feeds visitors and people who Adela knows to be destitute, pays for medical treatment for family members when she can, and spends a great deal of time minding and feeding a neighbor's children for free. Adela would laughingly tell me stories about gifts her daughter brought her from Puerto Rico. On one visit, she was given a ceiling fan to help keep her cool in the tropical heat. Adela, hating clutter, gave the fan away after a couple of weeks, her dislike of clutter being greater than her desire for luxury. Understandably, her daughter was quite annoyed and swore never to give her mother anything again. But she was mistaken in inferring that Adela is not interested in possessions at all. The things that Adela most values are mementos that represent her relationships with people she cares for: photographs of her family, a print of the Last Supper given to her by a cherished neighbor, trinkets that were given to her by her daughters, and drawings by her nephew Jeffrey. As Adela would regularly tell me, "Without family, you have nothing." After more than forty years in the barrio, Adela's family include the many people who have lived around her for all those years, especially constituted through her involvement with the Catholic Church.

A DREAM FOR GENERATIONS

Meanwhile, Cristino grew too old to finish his own home, and he left the task up to his sons, Marco and Felix. Marco's strategy has always been to build his own apartment above his parents' house, but to do so he first needs to finish their house below, where he is currently living:

> I'll put a concrete roof on and start constructing my house on top. I could rent my house on the second floor and live in this one below. Even if I leave La Ciénaga, if I have a house here my parents can rent it out and live more or less well. But the plan has always been to add a second floor that will be my house.

Second floors generally follow the same plan as the first floor, and are accessed by narrow external concrete stairs. These expansions of space are used prudently: they are either inhabited by an adult child and family, or rented out for extra income. Over the years I have witnessed the slow and steady transformation of Cristino's small dwelling from a wooden shack to a structure with concrete walls, an internal bathroom, a veranda, and bars on the windows. Working with Felix and occasionally paying a Haitian neighbor to help out, the family managed to construct a concrete floor, corner supports, concrete block walls at the front, and some concrete walls on the sides and internally. The front patio and Marco's bedroom have concrete ceilings, but the rest of the ceiling is tin.

Marco's brother Felix built his house in his parents' backyard, beginning when he was twenty-one years of age, not long after he married Veronica. It has grown considerably since I began fieldwork in January 2005, gaining a second floor and two extra bedrooms so that the three children do not have to share a room with their parents. For Felix, the construction of his house was made possible through his job in a hotel, his own ingenuity, and extensive help from his neighboring family and friends:

> My house is a small, modest house. I've tried to make it as comfortable as possible. I made it with my own hands. It has two levels, and I think the spaces are well distributed. At first I had planned to build a house with two levels and wooden floors. But it worked out that it would cost more, so I decided to construct completely in concrete block. When I started to build the house I didn't know anything about construction, so I started to investigate. I went to construction sites to observe how they do the work. I took measurements of how they placed the materials, for example, at what distance they put one column from the other. I started to ask people who worked in construction and took notes.
>
> Then in 1993, with the help of friends and my brother-in-law, we started to construct the house according to the research I had done. We started to lay blocks and we built the house. We did it between the family with myself as master builder. Although I had never laid a block in my life, we put my research into practice and I still believe that we achieved a good result. When other people come to see my work they asked me to work on their own houses. I helped Ariano

build his house because he collaborated here with me. But my first construction job was here.

Felix's pride in having constructed his own "comfortable" home echoes Holston's argument that autoconstruction counters negative representations of poor communities through "replacing them with new ones of competence and knowledge" (1991, 462). Achieving the material construction of a home is admirable given the heavy difficulties faced by the poor and proves that one is a *gente seria* (serious person) and a *gente de trabajo* (hard-working person), two often-cited categories of respectability. Physically building the house is therefore a powerful way of declaring oneself a person of skill and value.

By building his own house on his father's land, using inexpensive and readily available materials, and using his own and his family's labor, Felix dramatically lowered his building expenses. His family's living costs are also reduced since they do not have to pay rent, have no mortgage, and do not pay childcare (Felix's mother, Maria, looks after their three children while the parents are working). Felix's wife, Veronica, has worked as a cook and waitress in a large hotel for over a decade. For a few years they were looking for a place to rent in a more "organized" neighborhood, so that their children could be involved in extracurricular activities, but they did not manage to find a place that suited their budget. Plus, the move would take them away from family life and free childcare. Instead, in the last few years they have doubled the size of their house, adding on two bedrooms downstairs so that the three children no longer have to sleep in one large room with their parents. Having now adjusted their material circumstances to take account of their growing family, it now seems unlikely that the second generation will move away anytime soon. As Felix said to me back in 2005:

> Our family relations are good because we have always shared our problems and happiness. In this sense it is good. We have always maintained contact. For a while I lived in another part of the barrio but I had to return. I missed being with them. My uncles Diego and Ariano also live close by; my aunt Adela has always lived near us. Where one goes, the rest go and it has always been like this. We haven't been able to disperse ourselves.

Hence desires for a new environment, often expressed by the younger generations, are held in check by the ties of family, which are literally cemented into place and not readily reproducible elsewhere. This is because autoconstruction provides both the capacity for family members to settle near one another and a built environment that encourages socialization. Almost all housing in the barrios consists of small, individual family dwellings that are in close proximity to each other and to the street. The only exceptions to this rule are two- or three-story houses whose upper stories serve as apartment blocks. Houses are not hidden behind walls, nor do people generally shut their front doors when they are at home. There is a culture of visiting, with neighbors dropping in and out of each other's houses all day long, from dawn until late at night. Street spaces and pavements are heavily populated with children playing ball games, people buying ingredients from **colmados** (grocery stores), and ambulatory vendors selling products. In fact, socializing in the streets is not just commonplace; it borders on sacred ritual. Every evening, residents bring plastic chairs out onto the street to catch the afternoon breeze off the river, play dominoes, and gossip. Most families in the central area of the barrio have been living there for decades. As a result, people know each other very well, and the whole arrangement makes for a very social environment, albeit one that can be decidedly noisy and disruptive. Felix jokingly complained that studying for his university degree was nearly impossible. Despite the fact that his house is located in his parents' backyard, he said that the minute he sat down to read a book, his friends would set up a domino table right outside his door, and pester him until he gave up reading and joined in the game. The idea that other people might desire solitude and quiet simply does not occur to the average Dominican, who is intent on making *mucha bulla* (lots of uproar). Felix dreamed of migrating to Canada, where it is cold and quiet.

Cienigüeros admire, and aspire to, the modern housing in middle-class suburbs, but they claim that life there is unsociable and boring. Since I had lived in a middle-class area before moving to La Ciénaga, many neighbors of mine asked me whether I found middle-class life to be lonely. In fact, when I carried out a survey of the barrio in 2005, one young woman commented to me, "There in Gazcue the people live well but they lock themselves up in their flats with bars. It's like living overseas!" While this comment seems misguided, given that wealthier

Dominicans have much greater facility to travel and be granted much-sought-after green cards, not to mention experience other advantages such as a far-more-regular supply of electricity, this woman's viewpoint is a common one. In this sense, La Ciénaga may well suffer from physical underdevelopment, but according to the barrio's residents they live better emotional and social lives.

HOUSING AESTHETICS AND RESPECTABILITY

Efforts to transform the house over time are not just about finishing it or making space for a growing family or a business. In fact, one could argue that the house is never truly finished, as occupants will always be improving some aspect of the house, whether it be adding an extension or changing the decor. This process has two dimensions: working toward social norms of what a house should be, and displaying the talents, taste, and competence of its designers and decorators. While barrio residents have a low consumption capacity and are therefore limited in the status displays they can engage in, they nevertheless have one advantage over their equally poor neighbors renting elsewhere in the city. The labor, perseverance, and thrift they demonstrate by constructing their own house according to national ideals marks them as people of social value. They are the respectable poor who strive to get ahead, not deviants who threaten the social structure. As I explain in chapter 5, this moral-material discourse is partially used as a means of social control. However, social norms for what constitutes a respectable house are not necessarily set by an elite class. Many of the characteristics of the ideal house appear to be a national hybrid of urban and rural tastes, including basic style, paint colors, and decorations including paintings. Á la Bourdieu (1984), the tastes of the wealthy define what it means to have a high social status, but they do not define what it means to be moral.

Within the home, autoconstruction draws on a range of stylistic influences. Creativity is most visibly expressed through the colors of one's house. Dominican houses are notable for their palette of flamingo pink, lime green, bright yellow, deep red, and turquoise blue. A popular brand of house paint sells a range of "tropical colors" that are pre-mixed for Dominican tastes. While these colors are more commonly applied to single-level dwellings rather than blocks of flats, their pervasiveness throughout the countryside and the city means that they are accepted as a national style rather than a working-class or peasant style. They are part of the Dominican cultural landscape.

Creativity is also apparent in people's efforts to comply with norms despite a lack of resources. A sign of quality in a Dominican home is a tiled floor rather than a concrete one. When Marco was working with his father in the restoration of colonial buildings, he saved some old, broken Spanish tiles and took them home. He and Felix used them to tile the entryway to their parents' house, creating a beautiful and unique montage. In a similar manner, their mother, Maria, is creative in the placement of their furniture, regularly rearranging it within their small living space. Dominicans have a penchant for rearranging furniture on a regular basis to *cambiar el aire* (freshen the air). This exercise may seem futile among poor residents, who have little space and few material goods, but it creates an atmosphere of change and renewal without expensive purchases, and it allows them to use their limited space in new ways. A change in the arrangement of furniture always evokes entertaining comments from family and visitors on the skill and foresight of the arranger, as well as experimenting with the plasticity of the home's interior.

These practices can be compared to Trinidad. Daniel Miller (1994) writes that in contrast to what Bourdieu observed in France about the dominance of the elites in dictating style, Trinidadian households exhibit an aesthetic norm that crosses class, gender, and ethnicity. Competition exists in the displaying of material goods from a standard set, rather than in uniqueness of style. For example, mahogany furniture is an essential possession across the social spectrum, and even the smallest and poorest living room will generally have a couch with two mahogany chairs that are upholstered in the same fabric as the couch. It is not uncommon for these to be still covered in the original plastic for protection.

My observations in Santo Domingo are consistent with Miller's findings for Trinidad. Dominican social classes generally share ideas of what is good to have and good to be seen to have. While there are indeed aesthetic differences in terms of what people will display in their homes and wear on their person, these divergences seem minor compared to the conformity across classes. Mahogany furniture, floral china, and house fittings are standardized. Many of the differences boil down to a matter of economy of space. Since most living rooms in La Ciénaga are very small, they are usually crammed close together so that one has to move them or climb over them in order to sit down. Ownership of a set of shelves, a television, and a stereo is also normal, regardless of the condition and type of house or the income of its occupants. Shelves display ornaments, religious objects, and small vases with artificial flowers. Adela takes great care of her collection, though she often complains that she has *demasiado vaina* (a Dominican colloquialism meaning "too much rubbish"). She places all her ornaments on the upper shelves, where they are out of reach of small children.

As Miller (1994) found in Trinidad, differences in the interior decoration of middle-class and lower-class houses have more to do with income than style. Middle-class walls are decorated primarily with family portraits, certificates of achievement, religious pictures or slogans, and original paintings of Dominican rural or urban colonial landscapes. Lower-class walls are decorated in the same fashion, with the exception of original paintings. Instead, they display posters, pictures from magazines, calendars, and political propaganda. Neither class displays objects associated with Africa, such as Haitian paintings. Indeed, Haitian paintings are almost exclusively found in venues that cater to tourists, such as hotels and tour agencies.

The environment in which material items are embedded can have a strong impact on the status they convey collectively. Whether any given house is respectable or has high status depends upon its architecture, contents, the land it is built on, its use, and the people who reside in it. Concrete multilevel houses with spaces divided according to their function, bars on the windows, and air conditioning are highest in the architectural hierarchy, while small wooden ranchitos with only one or two rooms are the lowest. Internally, walls should be painted, surfaces tiled, and doors installed. Only a handful of houses in La Ciénaga have reached this state of distinction. Belgica's house is one of these. She is a long-time supporter of the church and a highly respected member of the community, works in the school cafeteria, and her husband owns a colmado. Her small house stands out from those around it because it has a concrete roof, its floors are completely tiled, all windows and doors are barred, and she has nonplastic furniture inside, including a matching sofa set and a dining table.

The house and its contents communicate volumes about a person's economic and social position, but it can also be misleading. While Belgica's house conforms to middle-class standards, she is clearly not a member of the middle class. Belgica's and her husband's incomes allow them to live well in La Ciénaga because they acquired land cheaply in the mid-1970s and do not have to pay a mortgage or rent. It took them three decades to develop their house to its present standard and acquire the material goods necessary to finish it. Most houses in the barrio started off at the most basic level and are in different stages of evolution, and so a family's housing style is often an indication of a longer residential period in the barrio rather than a reflection of their actual income.

Whereas in the beginning there were only ranchitos, the majority of houses in La Ciénaga are now made—at least partially—of concrete block, giving an air of heightened respectability to the barrio. On numerous occasions Adela pointed out to me with pride that nearly all the ranchitos on her street have been replaced with "good houses." The exception is her next-door neighbors, who have chosen to have their home re-covered in treated wooden planks, a cheaper and cooler solution. When Adela looks around her, she sees a settlement vastly different from the one she first occupied in 1972. It is far more populated, secure from evictions and the elements, with indoor bathrooms and all the modern, albeit irregularly delivered, services. Once a resident of farmland on the city's edge, Adela now finds herself to be very much an urban resident as a result of the passage of time rather than geographic relocation.

BUILDING THE FUTURE, LOCALLY

The desire to be urban was a major driving force for many residents' decisions to migrate from the countryside to Santo Domingo. They come to the city seeking an easier life and a better future for their children. Autoconstruction acts as a conduit to work toward these dreams. When I asked residents what their hopes were for the future, they almost universally responded, "Finish my house and get a good education for my children so that they can become professionals." These two projects, one of increasing economic capital (assets) and the other of increasing cultural capital (education), are intertwined: the house provides the security necessary to be able to give one's children a better education. The project of transformation thus spans generations. This is not so much a matter of putting hope on hold as it is recognizing the time involved in transforming life circumstances. The persistence of residents with their everyday activities is expected to have long-term pay-offs.

The house, apart from sheltering and nurturing the family, is an important economic resource that can be mobilized for far more than sheltering the family. Home businesses are common among women who do not hold regular employment. Women's work, paid and unpaid, is still predominantly centered on domestic activities. As Martínez-Vergne (2005) found in the late nineteenth century and Gregory (2007) in the early twenty-first century, women's work is often an extension of domestic work, with many women running small businesses from the home, working as maids in middle-class homes, or washing laundry. In Adela's small street alone there are at least six women's home businesses, selling a wide variety of products including bread, precooked red beans, jewelry, Avon products, and children's games.

A vast array of everyday consumption is also done locally in colmados, small grocery stores that are often located in a front room of a family home. They sell a large range of products, the staples being fresh bread rolls, mayonnaise, ham, rice, pasta, beans, basic vegetables, canned fish, cold drinks, and beer. Supermarkets sell most of these items cheaper than colmados, but are frequented less because they are further away and sell in larger quantities that many cienigüeros are unable to purchase. Rather than go to the supermarket to buy a can of tomato paste, a carton of eggs, and a pack of Maggi stock, residents will buy six pesos worth of tomato paste wrapped up in a small plastic bag, one egg, and a couple of Maggi cubes. Local businesses have a constant traffic of people making small purchases, partly because money is short, but also because of the barrio's proxemics in which people are always close to the street and the colmado may be no more than ten meters away. This consumer behavior is not entirely absent in apartment block communities such as Guachupita and La Caoba (where many cienigüeros were relocated to in 1977), but obstacles such as stairs and doors, and the need for keys, mean that this is not nearly as free-flowing, and there is more incentive to plan purchases. Of course, most middle- and upper-class households simply send the maid to do the shopping.

While the house is an important resource, it can also belie the struggles that take place to maintain everyday sustenance. A family may own a substantial and well-developed home, but struggle to make ends meet on a daily basis. Adela's nephew, Diego, is a good example of this kind of insecurity, as his large house conceals his family's poverty. Diego moved to La Ciénaga in 1998. He lives across the street from Adela with his wife, Sandra, and their six school-age children. As an adult, Diego studied three years of law but was unable to raise the funds to finish his final year of study.

> I spent fifteen years paying rent and it was difficult. At times I had to ask for an extension because in reality I didn't have the money, but thanks to God I now have a house and I don't pay rent. In 1995 Adela helped me start up a business selling music cassettes on the street. She lent me thirty-three pesos and I invested them in cassette tapes that I bought for one and a half pesos each and sold them at two tapes for five pesos.
>
> Then when I was presented with an opportunity of work I suspended my sales and I worked for a time in a shop. I spent seven years working and from the money I earned I moved to La Ciénaga and built the house I have now. My work paid an incentive for good work and with what I made I kept buying concrete blocks, buying blocks and laying them until thanks to God I could construct a level. Thanks to God I'm not paying rent. But when prices went up they had to let people go so I went back to selling music cassette tapes. The house still isn't completely finished; it lacks some details.

Eventually the spread of computers made copying music CDs inexpensive and Diego was no longer making much profit. He turned to selling mobile phone accessories on the street. His wife has worked as a domestic servant for years, earning 3,000 pesos per month (US$100). They live on the ground floor of their house. The second floor is divided into two apartments that Diego rents out intermittently to tenants for 1,000 pesos (US$25) per month for each apartment, and one of his sons, Wester (Adela's great-nephew), lives in a single room built on top of the house. In 2007, a businessman from outside the barrio rented out his small garage, installed a colmado, and hired Diego to manage it for 6,000 pesos (US$150) per month. Diego's salary is low and his working hours are very long, but he prefers the work to selling on the streets because it is less tiring and he is closer to his family. Despite having three sources of income—rent and two salaries—the household cannot always cover its expenses, especially struggling to pay their children's school fees:

> I have hopes to find a job, who knows if God will help me go a little more *adelante* [forward] and find a decent job. My children lack *el pan de la enseñaza* [lit. bread of learning] and food. I don't have anything to leave to my children because I am a man who is totally poor. We—my brothers and I—we don't have anything. Not one of us can talk about thousands of pesos because we don't have it. We have always been poor; none of us has ever lost a million pesos because we have never had it. But we are honorable people, and thanks to God we have never had problems with the law, nor anything similar, because if something doesn't belong to us we leave it there.

Yet the family members help each other. Adela has a personal mission of keeping Diego fed, as she knows that he will give his own food to his children. Diego points to economic crisis to explain his struggles:

> We are a humble family with wishes to *superación* [betterment] although life is difficult. Life has lately been hard for us with the high cost of living, with the high prices that have shot the *canasta familiar* [family shopping basket] to high prices, and one day's salary doesn't pay enough to eat well.

The economic situation compels many poor Dominicans to invent micro-entrepreneurial solutions, most of which fail to get off the ground due to lack of capital or lack of a market. For a short while, Diego tried selling medicine from the small shop at the front of his house where a neighbor used to run a bread shop. He set up a folding table with a variety of medicines displayed, from cough syrup through to painkillers and antibiotics. Diego's children staffed the shop while he continued to sell mobile phone accessories on the street. His three-year-old son, Max, was left in the care of the older children while his parents were at work, and he would often visit Adela's house to play with Morena's four-year-old daughter, Luisa. On one occasion, Max complained to Adela that his mother was at work. Adela responded, "But it's good that your mother is working! She works so that all of you can eat. It's a good thing!"

Diego does not see his house as having much value as an inheritable object because, like all cienigüeros, he lacks the title for the land the house stands on. Diego correctly identifies his house as the minimum requirement he and his family need to survive. Sandra dislikes La Ciénaga for its noise, pollution, and inconvenience, but they have little option but to stay where they are. The sale of the house would not buy the family much living space elsewhere in the city. This is a limitation that most residents face: building a house is a necessary strategy for securing a place and making a life, but the house alone generally does not provide class mobility or even a secure place in the market. It needs to be combined with other forms of economic, social, and cultural capital to provide enough leverage to make a difference.

Fortunately, extra forms of capital are becoming increasingly available to cienigüeros, evident especially in the number of young people attending higher education. Diego's son Wester studied information technology at a private university, paying for his tuition fees with money he earned working (figure 2.3). In 2012 he partnered with a more cashed-up friend to start the second Internet café in La Ciénaga, renting the front room of a house located across the road from his parents' home. The business is hand-painted with colorful logos of global brands such as Google and Firefox, telecommunications companies Orange and Claro, and game providers such as Nintendo.

Being a local is integral to Wester's business's operations in two ways: he has a ready-made network of clients who know and trust him, and he could leverage his connections and the barrio's low rents to secure a space for his business. In fact, it was thanks to local knowledge that Wester attended university in the first place: he was able to learn from older friends and family members who had trodden the path before him and could advise him on how to make his education happen. The benefits of autoconstruction and the close-knit socializing it encourages are not limited to providing homes or entertainment, nor are economic activities limited to providing just the most basic goods. La Ciénaga is a growing economy, increasingly connected to the city and the global world, whose consumption needs are changing fast. Local entrepreneurs readily provide new products and services for this changing demographic. In the next chapter I will describe how the state

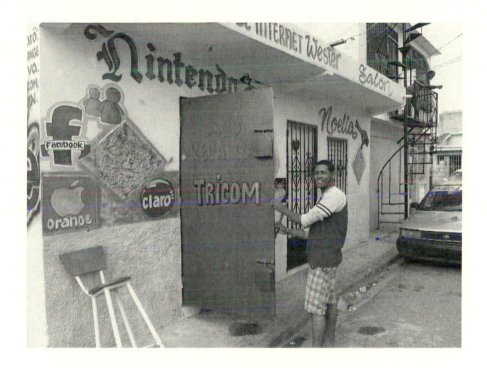

Figure 2.3. After studying computer science at university, Wester opened an Internet café in La Ciénaga in 2012. *Photograph courtesy of the author.*

resisted this urbanization for many years, finally coming on board in 1996 with the desires of cienigüeros for what they call progress.

3

TOO BIG TO IGNORE

The State and the Persistence of Squatting

> Those who command space can always control the politics of place
> even though, and this is a vital corollary, it takes control of some
> place to command space in the first instance. —Harvey 1989, 234

Night had fallen and for once the electricity supply to La Ciénaga was functioning. It came on just before the eight o'clock soap opera, arousing cheers of *llegó la luz!* (the light arrived!) from residents who were passing time socializing with neighbors on the street by the light of candles, kerosene lamps, or a battery-powered phase inverter. People immediately jumped to life, snuffed flames out, and switched on the television or stereo. Competing sound sources pumped reggaetón and merengue into the street.

In the sparsely starred night sky appeared a Christian cross, etched in light. It was the beacon of the Faro a Colón (or Faro), the inland "lighthouse" built by President Balaguer in Santo Domingo's west to honor the 1992 quincentenary of Columbus's arrival in the Americas. Its symbolism is unmistakable: it reminds observers that Dominican national identity is European and Catholic. The cross is also a mnemonic for the nation's long quest for modernity. The Faro was constructed on land usurped from the poor as part of a larger project to ready the nation for its moment of quincentennial glory. Residents were also to be evicted from the squatter settlements around the Ozama River, but the targeted communities are still there today. Occupying prime land by the river and close to the city's center, their locale could be worth billions of dollars if developed (Fay and Wellenstein 2005).

La Ciénaga was one of the communities targeted for modernization in 1992 as it occupied a portion of this valuable land and was considered an eyesore for people entering and leaving the city via the twin Bosch and Duarte bridges. It survived as a community for the poor through a combination of state ineptitude, local protests, and accidents of circumstance. Below the Faro's beacon and under the bridge, La Ciénaga serves as a reminder to both its own residents and the entire nation that shared developmental goals are still a long way from being realized. Yet residents and nonresidents do not always agree on how to reach their shared goals. Although cienigüeros desire development and modernity, they have also resisted outsiders' efforts to dictate the terms upon which it is achieved.

In the previous chapter, I argued that squatter settlements use the resources they have at hand to create meaningful lives in surprising ways. However, no analysis of material culture and poverty would be complete without addressing property rights and the means by which they are upheld. Residents of Santo Domingo's squatter settlements have struggled over the decades to gain material security and formal recognition. At times these have been classic political struggles to recognize land rights; at other times, residents have voluntarily participated in the state's push to dismantle the barrios entirely.

Yet one thing persists: people continue to move into the barrios and construct houses, despite the efforts of the state to halt the process of urbanization and the desires of residents to move elsewhere. This persistence rendered the barrio "too big to ignore" (Tett 2009): the state can no longer reclaim the land for development, because relocating its twenty thousand-odd residents is an economic and political impossibility. Cienigüeros have literally built themselves into the landscape despite their own ideals and the state's wishes. The political outcomes of squatting, its struggles, and its ultimate permanency, are realized less through ideology and protest, and more out of everyday material practices constituted over time and in space.

HISTORIES OF EXCLUSION

The exclusion of poor barrios from state visions of modernity has a long history. Dominican elites and intellectuals have viewed inner-city slums as impediments to progress since at least the late nineteenth century. Martínez-Vergne (2005) describes how, in the late 1890s, the Dominican urban elite, comprised of intellectuals, politicians, and a burgeoning middle class struggled to consolidate their power over the recently independent nation (see Bosch 1992). The year 1865 marked the Dominican Republic's second attempt at independence, having briefly returned to Spanish rule in 1861 after its initial independence from Haiti in 1844. The political and intellectual elite shaped nationalism around notions of democracy and progress, calling for the implementation of "modern agricultural techniques, secular education, and political participation as the cornerstones of the new nation" (Martínez-Vergne 2005, 1).

This idea of progress was based on European liberalism and would ideally be inclusive of all Dominican citizens, but "men of letters and men of state did not trust the capacity of the subalterns to make educated judgments about their own, let alone the country's, future" (Martínez-Vergne 2005, 50). They particularly wished to bring the "unruly" countryside under the state's control, a task made difficult by the dominance of **caudillo** (strongman) political leaders with their own private armies (see Wolf 1967). Urban elites considered the countryside to be a site of moral degeneration due to its lack of central leadership (Martínez-Vergne 2005). Large urban centers such as Santiago and Santo Domingo were chosen as the sites in which modern citizenship would be carved out. However, the urban working class presented a significant obstacle to the maintenance of order even in these "civilized" spaces:

> For municipal authorities intent on improving the quality of city life, these populations represented serious obstacles to their goals. They circulated freely around the city, presumably cared little about their personal appearances and hygiene, exhibited "scandalous" behavior, and thus strained the resources available to their superiors and public authorities to manage their existence. (Martínez-Vergne 2005, 127)

New municipal ordinances covered a range of social, economic, and aesthetic ideals, including implementing construction codes, banning animals in the city, regulating dance halls, and taxing stallholders in public markets. Social classes were spatially segregated, occupied different grades of dwellings, and socialized in distinct venues. Urban legislation and policies to separate the poor were increased during the dictatorship of Rafael Leonidas Trujillo from 1930 to 1961. Taking advantage of the damage wrought by Hurricane Zanón in 1931, in which Santo Domingo was virtually flattened, Trujillo removed all of the residents from inner-city slums to the *zona norte* (the northern zone between the city center and the river) to make space for the construction of wide, Paris-style avenues. He planned model suburbs complete with detached houses set back from the street to shift socializing from streets to private spaces. Trujillo built bridges to expand the city and monuments to emphasize the importance of past heroic events to the nation (Derby 2009). He also mobilized state historians, government departments, and the media to develop and disseminate a particular brand of national identity based on ***dominicanidad*** (Dominicanness), which presented Dominicans as being more European than African in an attempt to disassociate its history from slavery and blackness. Part of this *blanquimiento* (whitening) of the nation involved replacing the term *mestizo* (mixed) with the term ***indio*** (indigenous). The term *indio* infers that Dominicans are descended from the indigenous Taíno population. This is a work of fiction in application to Dominican society, because the indigenous population was largely wiped out by the 1530s (Knight 1990; also see Torres-Saillant 1998). However, it was a useful way for the state to avoid the politics of *mestizaje* (mixed race) and distance the country from Haiti's poverty and blackness. To keep the city civilized and as white as possible, migration from the Dominican countryside to the major cities was restricted, and public spaces were designed to serve the light-skinned elite. Migration to the cities boomed after Trujillo was assassinated in 1961, despite the fact that Joaquín Balaguer's subsequent presidencies (1966–1978 and 1986–1996) continued to dissuade rural to urban migration. President Balaguer issued a series of decrees banning migrants from settling in the zona norte to which they had been displaced by Trujillo, and reinforced the blanket ban against settlements in the swampy areas around the river, including La Ciénaga. With nowhere else to go, however, he was unable to stop the tide of settlers. Today, roughly half of the Dominican Republic's poor live in urban areas (Fay and Ruggeri Laderchi 2005, 41).

The flow of labor to cities and towns in the Dominican Republic followed a pattern similar to that of primary cities throughout Latin America as agricultural export income was overshadowed by income from IFZs, tourism, and international remittances (Portes, Dore-Cabral, and Landlolt 1997). When sugar prices dropped in the late 1970s, opportunities for wage labor also diminished. Land was scarce and rural communities were underserviced, so migration to the capital was an attractive option despite the government's hostility to the urban poor. Although Santo Domingo was not an industrial city, it was a growing global city with an important port that provided a range of low-skilled employment opportunities. Forms of employment in the 1970s were similar to those today. For women, they included work as domestic servants, factory laborers, and store clerks. For men, they included construction, street vending, transport, and limited work in factories (see Safa 1995). More recently, growth in tourism has resulted in an increase in jobs for tour guides and hotel workers. However, the Dominican Republic's cities and towns are nowhere near as readily marketable for mass tourism as are the resort zones of Punta Cana. Tourism has therefore provided limited employment opportunities in the major city centers.

Rural to urban migration increased rapidly from 1985 when IFZs began appearing in many Dominican towns. These zones give foreign companies tax incentives and duty-free access to the U.S. market. They are the result of the Caribbean Basin Initiative of 1984 and the rapid inflation of the Dominican peso, which lowered labor and other costs (Ferguson 1992). Santo Domingo has two major IFZs on the eastern and western margins of the city. Residents of Santo Domingo generally do not work in the IFZs unless they live very close by, because the cost of daily transport makes factory work economically unviable. Santo Domingo has therefore never truly been an industrial city, but rather a port and service center. The fluctuating fortunes of this type of economy mean that Santo Domingo has become what Trujillo and Balaguer tried so hard to avoid: a city with a population that is highly stratified along lines of class and race, with distinctly poor and wealthy areas.

The three main types of neighborhoods in Dominican cities are barrios, *residenciales*, and *ensanches*. Residenciales are secure apartment blocks that have locked entrances, bars on all windows, and often security guards at night. They are the main form of residence in the city center and are inhabited primarily by the middle class. The poor consider them the best place to live. Felix explained to me, "The residenciales are tranquil because you have to show identification to enter and there is a high level of security. You can sleep outside if you want and wake without fear in the morning that [anyone] is going to come and attack you." The third type of neighborhood, the ensanche, borrows from a word that means "widening" and refers to suburban developments characterized by open spaces, detached houses, modern services, and small parks. The ensanches in the east of the city are inhabited by the middle class, while those in the north are inhabited by the upper class. Whereas Trujillo's housing policies encouraged the expansion of middle-class communities across the river to the east, the upper class sought refuge in the north of the city, where they are sandwiched between lower-class neighborhoods.

There is evidence that spatial polarization has declined in recent years as a result of the development of factories on Santo Domingo's periphery (Portes, Dore-Cabral, and Landloldt 1997). The two major manufacturing zones to the east and west of the city blocked further expansion of the middle class, requiring different classes to reside more closely to one another. Proximity to the city's main features is little indication of wealth. David Howard argues that "social and economic exclusion rather than residential segregation characterize Dominican society" (Howard 2001, 66), indicating how type of housing and access to services (such as water, electricity, and education) are more reliable indicators of wealth and status than distance from the center of the city or even water views. There are still distinctly poor and wealthy residential areas, but they tend to be scattered in pockets throughout the city instead of clustered together.

The barrios around the Ozama River are arguably the most visible pockets of poverty in Santo Domingo due to their visibility from the city's bridges. Services to the approximately three hundred thousand people who reside in them (Fay and Wellenstein 2005, 97) in these areas are irregular and many sections are dangerous:

> Santo Domingo's central city slum spans several worlds, with varying vulnerability to flooding and landslides. When it rains, the risk of

flooding ranges from 6 percent for households on higher, consolidated ground to 45 percent for households near the river or along the main drainage systems and cañadas (gullies). Knowledge is common about which areas of the neighborhood are at risk of landslides. Rents (actual or imputed) reflect location safety and are almost twice as high in the safer areas than near the river or gullies. Housing quality also reflects risk perception, with simple wooden shacks in areas at risk for regular, catastrophic floods and multistory homes of durable materials in the consolidated part. (Fay and Wellenstein 2005, 103)

The barrios also pose higher-than-average health risks, including mosquito-borne diseases due to poor drainage and proximity to the river, disposal of sewerage into the river, and other water contamination. Barrio residents contrast the morality and healthiness of rural life with the corruption and pollution of the city, claiming that they would prefer to live in the countryside but it is an economic impossibility (see also Taylor 2009a):

Sometimes I'd like to leave because when one sees things like Cyclone David one wants to live in the high part, but in many ways this is the best area because it's so close to the city, this La Ciénaga. But it's not a good barrio anymore. And at times it's my wish to leave here to live again in my [family's] village in La Vega. One lives well there. But the church is here and I'm comfortable; the community in my village isn't like this one. This country dominicana is in darkness all over because the power plant isn't functioning. It's not like this in your country, is it? The light never fails there. (Felix)

Felix's comment reveals the tensions and ambiguities involved in the negotiation of place in modernity. His is a vision that looks inward to an idyllic past as well as outward beyond national borders. It is the city's poor that struggle most to resolve this dilemma, compelling them to be creative in developing their barrio from its rural beginnings to a community worth living in.

FROM EL CAMPO TO EL BARRIO

When people began to settle La Ciénaga in the 1960s and 1970s, they did so against a state decree that attempted to keep the land around the river free from settlement. In the early years, however, people like Cristino and Adela were able to develop their plots of land without state interference. During the three decades in which the Dominican government was failing to deal with La Ciénaga's existence, residents constructed an entire town. They not only built houses but also planned streets, constructed stairways, a park, a basketball court, and a school. In response to the growing population's consumption needs, entrepreneurs built a salami factory, an army of grocery stores, various garment workshops, salons, evangelical churches, beauty parlors, betting shops, bars, kindergartens, Internet centers, and a cock-fighting ring. Community organizations opened up headquarters in rented houses or rooms. Entire families relocated from the country to this new and growing community, cooperating to build their homes and survive through hard times.

Over the decades, urban residence changed migrants' lives, though adjustment was often difficult in the early years. The youngest child of eight, China moved to La Ciénaga before any of her family members, and convinced all of them to follow her over the next decade or so. She moved with her **marido** (common-law husband) into the neighborhood in 1973, when she was a young woman of nineteen years of age. China and her marido were already living in Santo Domingo, but had only recently arrived from the south. She had begun to collect building materials, such as sheets of tin, in the hope of finding a plot to build a house. When she heard about La Ciénaga from her father, she immediately secured a block of land. China told me:

> La Ciénaga was good. It was bad that there were so many mosquitoes and frogs. There were many, many, many of those, and we had so many crabs. Oh, la! Every morning we would fill a bucket with crabs that we collected in the house, running over the wooden floor, the zinc roof; we found them in all corners of the house. If I left the door open at night they would run into the kitchen; it was all full up with crabs. La Ciénaga wasn't so tremendous, but it was very quiet. There was a military base nearby and I slept with the door open, I never closed the door. I wasn't afraid.

Unlike Adela's perception of a threatening natural landscape, China (who arrived just one year after Adela) relates stories of frogs and crabs with a great deal of humor and reveled in the new community's *tranquilidad* (peacefulness). Interestingly, where Adela saw the military as a threat to the construction of her home, China views the military as the very thing that kept the new community safe. In fact, despite La Ciénaga's drawbacks, and various difficulties she has faced since, China is still fond of La Ciénaga as it fulfilled her dreams of building a house of her own. In the early years, her husband was away often as he drove trucks around the country. China, keen to earn extra money to invest in the construction of her house, began selling lottery numbers on the streets in Santo Domingo's commercial district, "turning black in the sun" from the long hours she spent outside. Her husband did not want his wife to work at all, so she did so in secret. Eventually they separated, and a friend convinced China to migrate with her to Switzerland. She spent a few years there washing laundry and returned to Santo Domingo with enough money to finish her house and buy another next door. Today she survives on the rent from this neighboring property and some assistance from her children, though she appears to help others more than receive money herself. Seven of her siblings still reside in the barrio, as do numerous nieces, nephews, and children, and the family socializes together extensively (figure 3.1). While there are other things she would like to achieve in life, such as returning to Switzerland to visit her friends, China's story is undoubtedly one of success in the face of immense hardship.

Whereas China's difficulties in adjusting to life in La Ciénaga were primarily economic (her own lack of resources and lack of state-supplied services), other people faced difficulties adjusting socially. Most settlers in the late 1960s and early 1970s came, like Adela, from the Cibao valley in the center of the Dominican Republic (which includes the ex-capital city of Santiago). They were predominantly Catholic, indio-colored descendants of European settlers, and were affronted by the blackness that characterized poverty in the city's margins:

> When we arrived in La Ciénaga it was a disaster. There were very few houses or people. We were afraid because we thought that it wasn't a good place, that it was bad, because there were very few white people around here. We were afraid because we were accustomed to seeing people like us.

Figure 3.1. **China plays dominoes with her family and friends on the street in La Ciénaga.** *Photograph courtesy of author.*

When Adela says that there were "very few white people" in La Ciénaga, she is not just referring to skin color. Adela herself is not "white" by Dominican standards, was married to a ***moreno*** (brown) man before moving to La Ciénaga, and has had a consistent stream of close friendships over the years with Haitians and Dominicans who Dominicans would describe racially as ***prieto*** (pitch black), ***negro*** (black), moreno, or *indio oscuro* (dark Indian). I learned over time that when Adela was referring to a person using a racial term, she was not necessarily referring to their appearance at all. In fact, she often seemed to be referring to where the person came from: were they from Cibao, where there the population was indeed somewhat lighter-skinned, or from near the Haitian border, where people tended to be darker? These regions were viewed as distant and culturally distant places. A new resident in the city and faced with a geographically diverse population, Adela was not sure how to cope socially with her new environment. Her fears were exacerbated in the late 1970s, and throughout the 1980s, as a new wave of migrants arrived from the south (geographically the southwest of the country), next to the Haitian border. Migration from Pedernales was propelled by a faltering agricultural economy in that region, lack of other employment opportunities, and damage wrought by Hurricane David in 1979. This was a time of industrialization in Santo Domingo, but it is unlikely that these particular migrants came to Santo Domingo to work in the zona francas as they are located at some distance from La Ciénaga. The majority of migrants took up employment in the traditional occupations of street vendors, domestic servants, and construction workers. The new migrants settled in the spaces that were formerly used for agriculture and filled the swamp with refuse to reduce flooding and construct houses on top of it. By the early 1980s, Cristino and Adela had given up their farmland to these newcomers. This second wave of migrants rapidly filled the vacancies left by dislodged families and virtually every other vacant space in the barrio as well:

> The poor have continued arriving from the country and the only opportunity they've found has been around here. You know that the poor can't live close to the rich, because the rich stop them. But when one moves to the poor barrios it's because there is a family of poor who can protect them and accommodate them. In this way La Ciénaga has been growing and now it's a town. (Angelo)

Angelo's comment suggests migrants to Santo Domingo had little choice but to settle in La Ciénaga. Nonetheless, in many ways they found it to be a welcoming environment. This was facilitated by the fact that many of the early residents encouraged other family members— parents, siblings, children, and cousins—to move to La Ciénaga. Lacking the resources to live in a more respectable, better-serviced part of the city, residents constructed a "family of poor" in which social relations could turn the barrio into a community of their own and partially compensate for their socioeconomic marginalization.

Today, approximately 60 percent of La Ciénaga's residents originate from the south, 22 percent from the agricultural region of Cibao, and just 5 percent from the southeast, the country's largest tourist region (Tejeda 2000, 33). There is a sizable group of Haitian migrants and their Dominican-born children, but few foreigners from other countries. Color differences between the waves of migration are noticeable as you move around the barrio, with slightly lighter-skinned people residing in the areas of the barrio arriba (the high land near the entrance and the central zone), and somewhat darker-skinned people residing in the areas abajo (lowlands prone to flooding). The shading of residential space is subtle but nonetheless real for residents.

Geovanny is one example of a migrant from the south whose urban experience has been overall beneficial. She was in her late teens when she came to La Ciénaga with her mother, América, in 1985:

> I came here because in my town, San Juan de la Maguana, there are very few opportunities. One leaves one's town looking for a better life. There in my town it is clean, more hygienic, because there isn't mud like here in La Ciénaga, but there is no way to survive. Here you find work more quickly for your family. There in San Juan there isn't any. The only thing to do is shell beans. They call it the granary of the south and work is seasonal.

Geovanny's view of country life as healthy but austere made them reluctant to move to the city. When their home was destroyed by Hurricane David in 1979, they spent a few years in temporary accommodation before migrating to La Ciénaga. Geovanny's mother, América, set up a **comedor** (food stall) in the streets of Santo Domingo, but she did not have a vendor's license and lost everything when it was confiscated by the military. In disgust, she retreated to her ranchito in La Ciénaga to sell lunch to bachelors from her home. She supplements the meager income this generates with sales of Avon products. América's son, who is an engineer, bought her a house. Geovanny lives with her husband and their three children and, in 2005, was earning a small wage as secretary for a community organization called **CODECI** (Coordination for the Development of La Ciénaga). Her brother's success as an engineer, coupled with her experience working with community organizations, inspired her to finish her secondary education and attend university. In one sense, Geovanny's current aspirations stem from a combination of witnessing her neighbors take up the opportunities that the city has to offer, and helping the community to organize internally and in its relations with the state. As Holston (1991) noted in Brazil, political struggles can bestow residents with skills in negotiating with the state and reimagining their own position relative to society. However, Holston also noted that residents of Brazilian favelas tend to give up their political activism once they have secured title to their land. I would argue that his observations hold true for Santo Domingo's barrios: political struggles aim not to contest its power, but to agitate for inclusion within it.

LA CIÉNAGA AND THE STATE

Negotiations between cienigüeros and the state began in earnest in 1977, when Balaguer issued a decree declaring the land around the river uninhabitable due to its tendency to flood. He sent in the military with the task of evicting all residents of La Ciénaga and neighboring Los Guandules, and clearing the area of housing. It was to become a recreational green belt protecting the river. Balaguer's government had constructed brand-new, concrete apartment blocks in Las Caobas, a suburb on the far western border of the city, to house residents of La Ciénaga. Many people, including Cristino and China, were disappointed not to be reallocated to one of these apartments:

> I was very sad when they didn't give me a house, because I truly wanted to leave here. I like my Ciénaga because it was here that I built my first house. They didn't give me anything, but I wasn't going to die of disappointment, right? I said to my husband, "What are we going to do?" So here we stayed. (China)

However, other people were strongly averse to relocation. For residents who worked in the city, the distance and cost of transport were serious obstacles, while relocation would mean loss of established clientele for those with home businesses. At the time, there was very little in Las Caobas except for the government's new apartments: no shops, no community, and very little public transport. While Cristino was prepared to commute the hour and a half it would take him to get to work, Adela would have struggled to make a living. Her ironing work required proximity to established clients, and it would have been difficult for her to sell products from home if she were surrounded by strangers and living on the third floor of an apartment block. The apartments in Las Caobas represented a very different style of social life to La Ciénaga's populated streets: more modern and private, but also more socially isolated. Today, Las Caobas is a pleasant, quiet neighborhood that is connected to the city by cheap, air-conditioned government buses that run along a well-maintained highway. At the time, though, there was no way for residents to tell whether the program would bring a net benefit or loss.

As things turned out, few people had a choice: some of those who wished to go, stayed; and some of those who wished to stay, went. Like many government policies, the relocation project sounded good in theory, but in practice failed to live up to its promises. Rather than an orderly transition in which all cienigüeros were allocated a government apartment and given a reasonable time to decide whether or not to accept, the program was characterized by poor planning, lack of communication, protests, corruption, and violence. Although the barrio was originally supposed to be vacated completely, the process of evictions soon became selective, with many of the better houses being left alone and only the wooden ranchitos destroyed, particularly those around the edge of the river. Cristino's, Adela's, and China's ranchitos were all located in the high ground and remained untouched. Cristino's son Felix recounts the events of 1977:

> My family was one of the unfortunate ones that weren't taken out of La Ciénaga in the evictions of the 1970s. Many people were taken to Las Caobas, a place with a certain level of comfort, but we weren't relocated even though my uncle [Daniel] was the director of the evictions, but he focused his preoccupation on the people closest to the river because it was assumed that they were in the most danger in case of floods.
>
> We weren't beneficiaries because it became a business in which those without money were not **desalojado** [dislodged]. They also sold apartments that were assigned to people in La Ciénaga. When this happened my uncle was no longer working with them; he wasn't a person who would do that. So, many people who were supposed to be relocated were left here. They were going to remove people from the eastern side of the river and also La Ciénaga. They cleared the eastern part completely without problems, but when they came here it fell into a state of disorder.

In Felix's view, his family missed out because corrupt officials commandeered Balaguer's orderly relocation plan and turned it into a business. He told me that in some cases, families bribed the military to let them stay in La Ciénaga; in others, military officers appropriated apartments meant for residents and rented them out to strangers. In other cases people sold their apartments and moved back to the riverside hoping for a second chance and another profit (**CES** 2004). Ultimately, Balaguer's relocations failed to achieve their purpose of clearing settlements from around the river (Santana 2004). In 1978, Balaguer lost the presidential election to Antonio Guzmán of the Dominican Revolutionary Party (**PRD**), and the evictions were put on hold indefinitely.

The evictions of 1977 prompted the creation of the Neighborhood Rights Defense Committee (COPADEBA) in 1979. COPADEBA began as an alliance between community organizations and grassroots Catholic groups in a number of barrios around the river. It also included labor unions, displaced families in the north of the National District, and NGOs. COPADEBA's objective was to challenge government displacement of poor people and seek redress for families whose homes were bulldozed without them being provided with alternative accommodation. It quickly became the biggest popular organization in Santo Domingo (Ferguson 1993, 570), and it still tries to maintain representatives in each of Santo Domingo's poor barrios.

La Ciénaga was largely forgotten after Balaguer's electoral loss to Guzmán in 1978. It was clear that the governments of Antonio Guzmán (1978–1982) and Salvador Jorge Blanco (1982–1986) were preoccupied with a series of political and economic crises and were not interested in resolving the problem of La Ciénaga. Neither helped nor hindered, the barrio continued to develop, receiving the majority of its migrants during the 1980s. Throughout these years of state absence, COPADEBA filled some of the gaps left by the state's absence, working actively in the barrios to improve living standards and represent the poor. They coordinated community activities, such as fixing the wall of the barrio's main drainage channel, and they ran training workshops in leadership and other political skills for barrio residents. COPADEBA now focuses its energy on gaining land titles for La Ciénaga's residents. The entire community is at the center of a court case with the Vicini, an Italian family who used to own large tracts of land in Santo Domingo. The Vicini claim that Trujillo illegally seized this land from them, while the Dominican state argues that the land was transferred legally. Today, there is little threat of eviction and COPADEBA's direct role in the barrio has diminished, but La Ciénaga's current level of internal organization is by and large due to COPADEBA's role in raising political awareness during those formative years. Their activities also meant that when Balaguer returned to power in 1986 and sought to continue his eviction policies, La Ciénaga had the numbers, the knowledge, and the networks required to implement some organized resistance.

MODERNIZATION REVISITED

Balaguer's return to power precipitated a new project to modernize Santo Domingo in time for the 1992 quincentenary. It also heralded a new wave of evictions for Santo Domingo's poor. Celebrations were to include distinguished guests such as the Pope, and its purpose was to remind the world of the Dominican Republic's historical importance as the oldest settlement in the Americas. The jewel in the crown of Balaguer's project was the construction of the Faro a Colón, the massive building in the shape of a cross that is located on top of a hill in eastern Santo Domingo. According to James Ferguson (1992), almost two thousand families were evicted from eastern Santo Domingo to make way for the Faro and its surrounding buildings. The project was criticized for squandering public funds that could have been better spent on development projects (Ferguson 1992; Krohn-Hansen 2001).

The Faro is not actually a lighthouse, but a massive tomb purportedly housing Columbus's remains. Krohn-Hansen interprets the tomb as symbolizing the state's memory of Columbus as "the most important ancestor of the Dominican people" (2001, 167). Its beacon was never meant to guide ships to safe port. Instead, it reminds Dominicans and visitors of the nation's Spanish-Catholic heritage. It is a monument to the Hispanic side of the Dominican Republic's past and represents the apex of the national project to convince the world that Dominican cultural roots lay with Europe and not with Africa. Part of the quincentenary project was to beautify the road from the airport to the city. This involved the relocation of the barrios that were visible from the Duarte Bridge. Felix explains:

> In the lead-up to the quincentenary of the discovery of America, before 1992, Balaguer wanted to clear La Ciénaga again because when you arrive via the bridge, what you see are all these *casuchas* [hovels]. Balaguer didn't want to see a barrio so disorganized right at the entrance to the city; he wanted to quit this image. He tried to

clear La Ciénaga again but he couldn't because it had grown too much.

In 1991, the military entered La Ciénaga again, this time to relocate residents to apartments in Cabayona and El Almirante, two suburbs in the north. Pimpina, a woman who lived in the flood-prone lower part of the barrio, describes how she was evicted:

> I was at home with the children and my husband was at work when the military came to our house. They gave us half an hour to pack up our things before putting us into a truck and carting us off to Cabayona, but there were no apartments left for us. When my husband came home from work nobody was there and the house was gone! They had knocked it down. Some neighbors helped him find us and we came back to La Ciénaga and constructed another house.

Pimpina and other residents recounted to me how the Dominican-born Jesuit priest and anthropologist Father Jorge Cela famously stood in front of bulldozers to stop houses from being destroyed and worked tirelessly to stop the evictions. Cela, who at that time was director of the CES, denies that he did anything quite so dramatic, but nevertheless he is remembered as a hero in La Ciénaga for putting his own safety at risk to help the people of the barrio. Adela commented, "Before Father Cela, we were nothing, we were just poor people. But Father Cela is a saint and changed things here." Indeed, Cela's role marks a turning point in the community's political memory. Before Father Cela, the Catholic Church played a background support role for organizations like COPADEBA, but from 1991 the church extended its influence in the barrio more directly.

PROPERTY AND THE PERSISTENCE OF PLACE-MAKING

The community was successful in stopping the evictions. The military response, however, was to blockade the barrio's main entrance. This was intended to prevent relocated residents from returning and prevent existing residents from bringing in building materials, furniture, and household appliances to reconstruct their bulldozed houses:

Balaguer put a military post at the entrance to try to stop people constructing more houses. The idea was that the military would stop people bringing in building materials and the barrio wouldn't keep growing, but the military let you bring in anything so long as you bribed them. So the blockade turned into a toll barrier and didn't work either. (Felix)

During the five long years that the blockade remained in place, residents paid the bribes demanded by the military or found other ways around it:

There was a very strong impediment; they wouldn't let us enter with things for the house and there were some very abusive officers. Where the marina is now [at the barrio's entrance], if we wanted to bring in a stove, we had to struggle. I have a son who was a lieutenant in the military but he couldn't help me. But I looked for another way in. We went by a street called Francisco del Rosario Sánchez and came in the back way. (Pimpina)

Lacking contacts with someone in power, Pimpina simply evaded the blockade. Dependence on social contacts is a recurring theme in stories about the evictions as neighbors or powerful people are called on to counter the ill effects of the state. The theme of cooperation is prominent in many accounts of these difficult years. However, a different view of the community's sociality can be seen in the comments of Maria, a young woman who was born in the barrio and trained to be a nun before studying law. Rather than focus on cooperation, Maria points to the ***corrupción*** (moral weakness) of individuals in destroying residents' collective chances for betterment:

Many people were selected for relocation. But if you go to the river you'll see that many people are still there. But why? Because the people who were relocated and given houses in the era of Balaguer were people who lived on the river, but they sold their apartments and returned here again. How are we going to resolve the problem? Well, never! Now there are no relocations because the government won't have anything to do with it. In all the barrios the people are bad; you give them an apartment and they look for more. (Maria)

Maria's argument is that because barrio residents have acted selfishly, taking more than their fair share, the government no longer wishes to help the barrios. The state's relocations were desirable, but the project failed due to the immoral acts of a few residents who derailed progress for all. This idiom of sociality and corrupción is also used to talk about the nation's past. Dominicans of all origins tend to agree that corrupción is a Dominican character trait that causes the nation to repeatedly fail to achieve political and social stability. The corruption of the Dominican character may be invoked to explain, and justify, long periods of violent rule in the past or justify police violence. According to this viewpoint, Dominicans are disorderly and need **la mano dura** (a heavy hand) to make them obey the law and work together for the good of the nation. Ideas such as these make many cienigüeros reluctant to denounce Balaguer's actions, even when his policies were unfair and a failure.

AFTER THE BLOCKADE

In some ways, the violence inflicted on La Ciénaga stemmed as much from its invisibility as its visibility from the bridge. Felix told me an amusing anecdote displaying the extent of the barrio's invisibility to the state. He said that in 1992, cienigüeros grew tired of the blockade and formed a group to protest outside the Presidential Palace. When Balaguer heard the noise, he asked an aide who the protesters were and what they wanted. When the aide replied, "They are the people of La Ciénaga," Balaguer exclaimed, "La Ciénaga? But it doesn't exist!" Balaguer had become blind between his two long stints as President (1966–1978 and 1986–1996) and could no longer see the site that had once annoyed him so much when he crossed the Duarte bridge. Nobody had told him that the forced evictions had failed to clear the area of housing, not least because the military personnel were making a large profit in bribes from residents who wanted to bring building materials and household goods to the barrio.

Whether or not the story is true matters little. It is indicative of the tenuous status of a barrio whose progress has mostly been achieved by flying under the radar of the state, but whose security and well-being ultimately depend on the state's recognition. Balaguer's military block-

ade of the barrio stayed in place until 1996, when Dr. Leonel Fernandez of the Dominican Liberation Party (**PLD**) was elected for his first
term as president. The barrio has changed dramatically since:

> In '96 Leonel arrived. We were struggling. We shouted and shouted
> for him to get rid of this impediment [the blockade], that he would
> help us. Then they gave us telephone lines, paved the streets, they
> put pipes for potable water and collected some of the sewage, be-
> cause this used to be a swamp full of crabs and trees. But with the
> arrival of so many people all the trees died, the people have cut down
> all of them and constructed many houses. We're already a town.
> (Pimpina)

Fernandez's government lifted the military blockade that had been
constraining La Ciénaga and instigated the first state projects to modernize it. Residents could again bring in building materials and furniture without having to pay bribes, and the government extended services such as running water, sewerage, and phone lines to the barrio. By
this time, the state had no choice but to recognize it, because its inhabitants had very much transformed it into a concrete reality:

> Leonel Fernandez arrived and ended the decree that prohibited this
> limitation on the people of La Ciénaga because he understood that it
> was impossible to dislodge a barrio that had more than fourteen
> thousand families. It was impossible because the government didn't
> have a housing project capable of accommodating all these people.
> So Leonel understood that it was better to invest in the barrio, and it
> was then that they paved the first streets, brought piped water to
> Clarín, and organized the electricity a little. This is the government
> that has invested the most in La Ciénaga. (Felix)

Fernandez visited La Ciénaga and launched a host of improvement
projects over the next few years. The federal government, together with
the European Union and local organizations, invested money in projects to make the area safer and provide more extensive and frequent
services. Projects have included installing telephone lines, paving
streets and alleyways, improving housing, installing indoor lavatories,
constructing storm water drains, increasing electricity supply, and
building a new school to replace the community-built structure that
sank in the swamp. The residents who benefited most were the minor-

ity who have street frontage, as services were not always extended to houses hidden away in the barrio's alleyways. Improvements were widely publicized by the media, and residents of other parts of the city became aware that things in La Ciénaga were changing.

Little happened in La Ciénaga under President Mejía from 2000 to 2004. When Fernandez was inaugurated as president for a second time in 2004, residents expressed hope that the new government would not only improve the barrio but also create greater opportunities for socioeconomic advancement at the national level. By 2009, there were indeed many more improvements to the barrio: a new storm water system installed to reduce flooding, new stairways, paved alleys, and an impressive children's park (figure 3.2). More recently, a bus service began running from the school and church in the center of La Ciénaga to downtown Santo Domingo and the Universidad Autónoma de Santo Domingo (Autonomous University of Santo Domingo, established in 1538). In 2011, the state began to force residents to pay their monthly electricity fees (of about 250 pesos, or US$6.50) and began to deliver a more regular supply of energy, with blackouts reduced from twelve hours per day to seven. La Ciénaga and its main streets appear on official maps of the city, and every street and alleyway has been sign-posted by the state. The only outstanding issue preventing La Ciénaga from being made into a fully formal neighborhood is the matter of land titles, which seems unlikely to be resolved any time soon.

A PLACE AT THE CENTER

La Ciénaga today bears little resemblance to the swamp that existed in the 1970s. Aesthetically, the transformation of housing, construction of streets, and beautification of public spaces has meant that the barrio easily meets minimum standards of what a working-class barrio should look like. Indeed, its centrality and the existence of features such as a large children's park and a small waterfront promenade are a form of material wealth, giving the barrio a significant lifestyle advantage over many other areas of the city. Abject poverty has also been significantly reduced. Far fewer residents live in dangerous and unsanitary conditions, due to the construction of storm drains, toilets, and the strengthening of houses against the elements. There are still areas of the barrio

Figure 3.2.   La Ciénaga's brand-new playground teems with activity soon after its inauguration in 2008. *Photograph courtesy of the author.*

that are in urgent need of development, including the river's edge and the central part of the barrio, where families are at risk of floods and landslides. A medical clinic and numerous public health programs are working to reduce rates of communicable diseases, improve pregnancy outcomes, and other projects. As I will discuss in chapter 5, crime has reduced and residents are subject to far less social stigma than when I first moved into the barrio in 2005. Increasing numbers of children are observing their parents' wishes to gain professional qualifications, although this can be a difficult task to fulfill due to inequalities in access to education and chances in the labor market.

However, these significant transformations have not necessarily resulted in a heightened confidence in barrio life or future opportunities. In August 2005 I was designing my survey of La Ciénaga and asked my neighbor, Marco, for advice. He took issue with one particular question I had included: "Would you move away from La Ciénaga if you had the opportunity?" Marco argued that this question was redundant, because every single resident would answer "yes." If they answered "no" they would be lying, because no sane person would choose to reside in La Ciénaga voluntarily. Indeed, when I collated the results of the survey, 96 percent of my three hundred respondents reported that they would leave La Ciénaga if they had a choice. Who, they argued, would want to live in a barrio marginado characterized by delinquency, pollution, and poor housing?

When I repeated the survey in November 2009, virtually all three hundred respondents said that the barrio had improved across the board. However, to my surprise, they seemed to hold *less* hope in the future than in 2005. After questioning a few people, I came to the conclusion that the main reasons for the loss of hope had to do with the current political climate and entrenched opinions about the barrio. Respondents for the 2005 survey were unhappy with the material conditions of the barrio and the high levels of delinquency in it, but expressed hope that Leonel Fernandez, less than a year into his second term as president, would improve their life chances significantly. Confidence in his government was especially high after the disastrous presidency of Hipólito Mejía from 2000–2004. His focus on education and technology as the way for the nation to progress seemed like sound policy to squatter settlement residents who viewed (and continue to view) education as a primary route out of poverty. While residents saw their own barrio transform, they did not consider that Fernandez had delivered on his promises for better education and a better national economy. Their disappointment was compounded by the near-universal view among cienigüeros that the barrio is antithetical to progress. While building one's own house provides shelter and security, and is a primary goal for vast numbers of residents, progress is almost universally considered to be something that happens outside the barrio, not within it. Locked into place, residents invest a great deal of time and energy constructing a locality while their hopes and dreams lie elsewhere (Taylor 2010).

Why, if the barrio has transformed so radically, do residents believe that barrio life excludes the possibility of progress? The obvious answer is that the barrio has experienced such a significant degree of poverty and stigma in the past that residents cannot help but associate the barrio with suffering and struggle. However, I suspect that the answer lies outside the barrio just as much as within it. The national history that

I briefly introduced at the beginning of this chapter gives us a clue to how Dominicans think about their own nation. While they are highly patriotic, they also view their country as one that is constantly at risk of failing to achieve progress for all of its citizens. Uniting the nation at the end of the nineteenth century through the exclusion of the poor, Trujillo's and Balaguer's treatment of "vagrants," the devaluation of the peso in 1984, the crime wave that followed economic crisis, corruption in politics and business—all of these historical events impacted the Dominican Republic's poorer sectors more strongly than anyone else. Hence La Ciénaga has improved overall in terms of security and wealth, but it is still poor relative to the rest of the nation, and it is also at the greatest risk of suffering during national crises. It is unsurprising that barrio residents, who were largely invisible to the state for years, have little faith that they will be beneficiaries of government investment in social goods such as education. Instead of faith in change driven by the state, then, they often place their faith in religion to deliver both spiritual and material benefits. In the following chapter I discuss how these two roles overlap.

4

¡CRISIS IS COMING!

Material Manifestations of Immaterial Ends

In a barrio such as La Ciénaga, all religion has a politics. This is not to argue that one's religion is a political choice, but that in circumstances of dire poverty and marginalization, religious practices and institutions have particular salience in people's lives. With little faith that the state, the economy, or a political movement will provide a safe passage out of marginalization, residents look to religion, which offers both spiritual comfort and opportunities to change one's material circumstances.

The politics of religion works through two channels in particular: the organizational structures of religion, and collective imaginaries of a moral community. Religious organizations, especially the Catholic Church, offer ways to engage with politics. Since the end of Trujillo's dictatorship in 1961, the Catholic Church in the Dominican Republic has backed the development of a wide array of civil organizations and advocated for state recognition of the rights of the poor, including the development of infrastructure and organization of the barrios. At times the involvement of the laity in the church's projects is overtly political; at other times it is indirect, characterized more by a trust in the church as an advocate for the poor. As Rowan Ireland has written of Campo Alegre in Brazil:

> The citizens in [these] communities were . . . prudent and anything but political revolutionaries. Nevertheless, they mounted an influential critique . . . of bureaucratic . . . authoritarian pretensions. . . .

Arguably, moral communities of this sort . . . are essential to any deepening of Brazilian democracy. (Ireland 1993, 63)

A similar observation could be made of Santo Domingo's barrios. For Dominicans who hold little faith in the ability of political processes to improve their life chances, religion provides a vision of an eventual redemption, and an alternative morality, one in which the poor are more blessed than the wealthy. Even residents who are directly involved in political action tend to be mobilized primarily around moral concerns. The Dominican Republic is not alone here: in the context of a global world where states and transnational markets operate in sync, religion has become a vehicle for worldwide reactions to poverty and dispossession (see Jameson 1998, 64). This gives a new meaning to the notion that religion has more than one "competence" (see Worsely 1968, xxx–xxxii) and, in Miller's (1994) terms, provides more than one "transcendence" or point of security in a fast-changing world.

Part of the reason why religion is so attractive is because it does not just provide an anchor in the present, but also a concrete vision of the future. In La Ciénaga there are two dominant visions of what the future holds. They are distinctly different in their end goals and they diverge markedly in their relationship with the material world. The first vision predicates the end of the entire material world through the second coming of Christ (the apocalypse). This vision is shared among the almost-universally Christian community, but it is particularly the domain of the Pentecostal churches. They preach that there is no worldly solution to the unfolding crisis, and encourage a turn away from the material world and consumption, in favor of a focus on God and the afterlife. However, their religious activities give the Pentecostals a strong material presence in the barrio, as religious services, hand-painted graffiti, clothing, vocal evangelizing, and churches are integral to efforts to practice their beliefs and communicate their vision. Furthermore, while their objectives may be apolitical and immaterial, their practices take place in the context of the barrio and reflect residents' marginal position in the socioeconomic hierarchy.

The second vision for the future proposes the end of the local material world—not by destroying or abandoning the barrio, but by transforming it into an ideal modern community through widening streets, demolishing shacks, creating parks, and so on. The Catholic Church, the state, and NGOs have all contributed to the barrio's transformation over the last few decades and have two concrete plans for a more thorough redevelopment. Such a transformation of the barrio's material form would radically transform its place in the city's social imaginaries: the community "under the bridge" would cease to be a symbol of urban poverty. However, these plans would require the relocation of large numbers of residents and a vast investment of resources, meaning that they are unlikely to be completed any time soon. In the meantime, the church encourages residents to become politically active and socially aware. Inspired in part by liberation theology, and in part by the need to compete with the global growth of Pentecostalism, the Catholic Church's aims are very much centered on socioeconomic development, the growth of civil society, and their own evangelizing. It preaches moral values, particularly centered on the household, as an antidote to the precariousness of urban life in the margins. Its morality does not entail the abandonment of consumption, but rather a reformation of values according to social imaginaries of an idyllic past.

Residents who espouse these visions of the future share the contradiction that the majority of their efforts go into transforming the material world while waiting for it to come to an end. Whether attempting to meet everyday needs, or aspiring to socioeconomic mobility, residents embed their lives, their hopes, and their sense of crisis within the material environment of the barrio. In the words of Manuel Vásquez, "practitioners' appeals to the supernatural, god(s), the sacred, or the holy have powerful material consequences for how they build their identities, narratives, practices, and environments" (2011, 5). I discuss these material manifestations and their implications for life in a very poor community while its residents wait for, work toward, or give up on different ends.

MATERIAL MEANS TO AN IMMATERIAL END

On many of the mornings I spent in La Ciénaga, I was awoken at dawn by the sound of a local woman evangelizing. She would tour the barrio on foot, warning residents that they had better reform by adopting Christ. "¡Siga Cristo!" (Follow Christ!), she would announce, delivering a sermon on the dangers of sin. Later the same morning she would walk past again, this time advertising that she was selling cooked red beans. On other mornings, when she was absent, a truck with a loudspeaker mounted on top would wind its way through the barrio, loudly broadcasting a pre-recorded tape with messages of liberation. The sound of these daily ablutions is very particular. Being lulled out of one's sleep by urgent proclamations of the end of the world has a bodily effect—physical as much as psychological—that tends to imprint itself on one's memory. Along with the roar of motorbikes, the sound of chatter, and the smell of coffee, it creates an experience of dawn that is particular to Dominican barrios.

These religious messages, such a feature of everyday life in squatter settlements, appear less frequently in other Santo Domingo suburbs. In wealthy Gazcue, working-class Sabana Perdida, or in the gentrifying suburb of Cristo Rey, it is far more common to hear pick-up trucks plying commercial wares. "We buy everything that is old!" announced one such fleet of pick-up trucks that would wind through the city daily. "We buy refrigerators, air conditioners, washing machines, everything old!"

Whether plying commercial wares or religion, the seller believes they have something of value to offer the listener. The urban poor, by necessity accustomed to fixing "everything old," are less likely to have a spare refrigerator to sell, but they do indeed have use for spiritual engagement. According to my 2005 survey of La Ciénaga, around 63 percent of residents are Catholic (around 12,000 people), 14 percent are Pentecostal (around 2,500 people), 13.6 reported no religion, 6 percent reported that they are Christian but did not define a denomination, 1.3 percent are Adventist, and 1.3 percent are Jehovah's Witness. Nineteen percent of residents say they attend church at least twice per week, and a further 15 percent say that they attend once per week. These numbers changed little when I surveyed the barrio again in 2009, and are similar to national figures cited by the United Nations High Commissioner for Refugees (2010). What is different about religion in La Ciénaga, compared to the rest of the Dominican Republic, is how it is practiced in the context of the barrio's poverty. In this chapter I will concentrate on the Catholic and Pentecostal communities, as they are the two largest and most visible groups.

Religion in La Ciénaga has highly visible material manifestations. In the houses of Catholics, the display of ornaments, calendars, and prints depicting religious figures speaks to the importance that residents place on religion in their everyday lives. This is not nationally consistent, either by location or by social class. I did not find the same prevalence of religious items in the homes of middle-class residents of Santo Domingo, nor were they common in the homes of residents of Pedernales, a town in the poorest region of the Dominican Republic that is located just two kilometers from Haiti. Pentecostals do not use objects of religious worship, but they may be identifiable by their form of dress. Women are encouraged to wear skirts, eschew makeup, and wear minimal jewelry or other adornments. Their back-to-basics look is particularly noticeable in the Dominican Republic, where fashions tend toward flashy displays. Mainstream trends, such as fingernails painted with elaborate designs, straightened hair, diamante-studded clothing and bags, are all widespread forms of adornment among women, especially among the younger generation. Dominican men also put in a great deal of effort to look good, including sculpting their facial hair, wearing sharp clothes, and carefully choosing accessories. Given the ubiquity of this kind of personal aesthetic, it is often easy to identify Pentecostals by their lack of adornment. Their efforts to differentiate themselves from the mainstream population are a clear communication of their religious identities and are a way to symbolically distance themselves from contemporary life.

Each religion's places of worship differ markedly. Whereas Catholic Mass is housed in one single church that holds a large congregation (figure 4.1), the Pentecostal churches are often tiny, numerous, and spread throughout the barrio. For many years, Catholic Mass was held in the local school's assembly hall. In 2008, a brand-new church opened across the road from the school. One cieniguero commented to me that the new church "belongs to another social class" because its impressive, airy structure looks out of place in the barrio's narrow, crowded streets. Inside, classic wooden pews seat the congregation, religious paintings line the walls, and Catholic artifacts such as candles and communion objects stand by for ceremonial use. The aesthetic and symbolic appeal of this new church has propelled average congregation numbers to increase from approximately 100–150 people when I was attending Mass in 2005, to around 500 when I was doing my second survey in November 2009, indicating that residents identify with the new structure's aspirational nature, rather than feeling alienated by its foreignness.

Conversely, the Pentecostal churches are generally small, one-room, concrete buildings that may be stand-alone structures or located in the front room of a house. They are identifiable by the names painted onto them more so than by their architecture. Inside, they are furnished with rows of plastic chairs, a loudspeaker system, some musical instruments, and perhaps a raised stage for the pastor to give his sermon.

The material differences between the two churches reflect their structures of governance: the Catholic Church is a centralized, global institution, whereas the Pentecostal churches are often disconnected, each one managed and funded by its own pastor. The largest Pentecostal church in my area consisted of a one-room, detached building with a floor area that was equivalent to that of a small house. It was run by a local man who at the time owned the only four-story house in the area. His home was perhaps fifty meters from his church, meaning that the

Figure 4.1.   The Catholic church in La Ciénaga opened in 2008. Mass was previously held in the school across the road. *Photograph courtesy of the author.*

pastor was in daily contact with his congregation, most of whom resided very close by. The pastor and his wife lived on the top floor of their building and rented out the other floors. The house was well finished, painted with embellishments, and boasted ornate balcony railings. For this pastor, the autoconstruction of his church had facilitated the construction of his home and the improvement of his socioeconomic position.

Both the Catholic and Pentecostal presence permeate street life. Besides holding religious services inside their respective churches, they also stage weekly services in public spaces. Every Thursday afternoon, the Catholic church holds Mass in the yard of a member of the congregation, rotating weekly around the barrio's six sectors. Given the public nature of private life in the barrio, these events are generally not at all hidden from view. Indeed, their point is to give the church visibility and increase attendance. They are also intended to demonstrate the church's commitment to the poor by taking Mass out of the church and into the yards and twisting alleyways of the congregation's worst-off members. These outdoor Masses are run by the congregation's leaders, who set up chairs, tables, and other props. They open Mass, lead the congregation in prayers, read bible verses, help the priest to administer communion, and at the end of Mass announce upcoming community activities. A Jesuit priest delivers the main sermon, wearing white vestments over his button-up shirt, jeans, and sneakers. Occasionally, if the priest is away, a nun will step in to give the sermon. The Catholic congregation also holds small weekly prayer meetings, almost exclusively attended by women who gather in a private home. Indoor Mass, held three times per week in the large new church, is more formal and more widely attended.

While La Ciénaga is predominantly Catholic, it is the Pentecostals who most saturate the senses of residents due to the enthusiasm with which they bring their proselytizing into the streets. The Pentecostals' outdoor *cultos* (lit. cult, meaning "religious service") tend to be more lively and spectacular than Catholic Mass. In fact, they are a form of barrio entertainment that attracts Pentecostals and Catholics alike. Once per week, the tiny Pentecostal church across the road from where I lived in La Clarín would put plastic chairs out on the street, set up a loudspeaker system, and hold boisterous meetings in the cool evening air. Pentecostal services are largely run by church members, and dozens of different ones are held throughout La Ciénaga and follow a similar format. The first part of the service lasts for around an hour and consists of the singing of hymns and Christian songs (by individuals or the group) to the accompaniment of the church band. The band consists of young men who play a synthesizer, a congo drum, and a *güira* (a Dominican percussion instrument). Cultos are very much a physical event: besides music, they feature glossolalia, fainting, dancing, and other physical performances, maximizing the use of the body's senses to increase the intensity of the experience (see Vásquez 2011). Their heightened aesthetic draws attendees into the moment, and also encourages the attention of neighbors on the street.

A number of Pentecostals explained to me that it was the music that inspired them to attend the church initially. Angelo, who runs a carpentry workshop in La Ciénaga employing three local young men, was enticed to convert to Pentecostalism through witnessing these public events. As he explained, "One day I passed by the church and I liked the rhythm of the music they had; the music attracted my attention, and after I continued attending until I stayed for good." Fortunately (because they are impossible to avoid hearing), few Catholic residents seemed to mind the **bulla** (noise) either: neighbors of all denominations gather to watch the preparations and stay for the entertainment, commenting to each other on the singing, dancing, musicianship, preaching, testimonials, and the occasional person fainting. The highly sensory nature of cultos brings to mind Fredric Jameson's (2005) comment that our imaginations of utopia are limited by our senses: our connection to the material world through touching, feeling, seeing, tasting, and smelling defines our transcendental experiences. Hence it is through the material world that we communicate our beliefs, structure our practices, and experience spirituality.

MESSAGES OF SALVATION

While aesthetic performances attract people to church, messages of salvation compel them to keep returning. Pentecostals put much more emphasis on the afterlife than the Catholic Church, communicating its importance through sermons, evangelizing, and a plethora of graffiti painted onto walls and signs (figure 4.2). Before the barrio's entrance was renovated by the government in 2009, one of the bridge's large pillars was painted with a scrawled declaration of *"¡Cristo viene, prepárate!"* (Christ is coming, prepare yourself!). The cliff that divides La Ciénaga from the rest of the city, which is reinforced with concrete to prevent landslides, has been adopted as a giant canvas boasting eight-foot-high letters spelling out "Cristo liberta" (Christ liberates). In the barrio's twisting alleyways, "Hoy yo sigo Cristo" (Today I follow Christ) is painted onto a roughly cut piece of particleboard and nailed onto a post.

Religious graffiti competes for attention with commercial advertising that is hand-painted onto the sides of shops, ranging from brand names that closely mimic a company's logo (such as Maggi stock) to more creative images of women wearing G-strings and strapless tops straddling giant bottles of Presidente beer (figure 4.3). Betting houses called *bancas* are colorfully decorated with the names of the games they sell and large dollar signs painted on their walls. Gambling, bling, sex, and

Figure 4.2. "Christ Liberates" and other religious slogans are painted on walls and signs around the barrio. *Photograph courtesy of the author.*

alcohol occupy an ambivalent place in Dominican cultural life, and are associated with a perceived moral crisis that has descended on the Dominican Republic since the economic crisis of the 1980s. To disassociate from this moral crisis, churches and congregations invoke a religious code to render La Ciénaga's pious as a moral community. According to this understanding, wealth is the cause of immorality, not the other way around. Maria, who spent a year studying as a novice in Santiago before returning to Santo Domingo to study law, commented of her fellow barrio residents:

> The poor are stronger believers. The poor look for a refuge in religion. It doesn't matter which religion, but they look for a refuge. The rich aren't like that. The rich look for refuge in their money, and at times, perhaps one day, they go to Mass. The poor no, the poor don't have any money so they look for something that fills them, and they put themselves in religion because they want to believe in something and the only manner to believe is to put yourself in a religion, whichever it is. There are many poor people who are rich in spirit; that's what I've always said.

Hence religion is not merely a matter of individual faith, but of social class. However, while this discourse reclaims some of the lost social status of the poor, it implies that seeking socioeconomic betterment is a dangerous moral path to tread, with the implication that increased wealth and consumption will lead to moral corruption. Adherents to this idea—that mass consumption is inextricably intertwined with immorality—appear to reject what Jean and John Comaroff call "millennial capitalism," meaning "a capitalism that presents itself as a gospel of salvation; a capitalism that, if rightly harnessed, is invested with the capacity wholly to transform the universe of the marginalized and disempowered" (Comaroff and Comaroff 2001, 2). For many barrio residents, religion continues to trump capitalism as the primary source of support and salvation. In fact, religion also trumps the state as provider of social goods and social order. Though the state was once highly effective in imposing order through violence, rising crime rates give locals the impression that the state has lost power since the demise of Trujillo and Balaguer. Instead, power and order are only to be found beyond this material world:

Figure 4.3. A colmadón advertises its products via this hand-painted sign of a woman riding a bottle of Presidente beer. *Photograph courtesy of the author.*

At times one asks God for something but God says that if one asks him you have to wait for the reward, and if he doesn't give it to you it's because it doesn't suit him. Every day you need to have more confidence in him because he is the only one that can help you in everything.

If you are going to go out, first you ask that everything will go well. You thank God for the bread that he has given you, for the water, the daily bread, also for the air, for nature. I also thank God for the name he has given me, for the strength he has put in me, because it is he who gives me the strength I need. Because look at the times we are living in, with so much wickedness, so much selfishness, so much injustice, so many things that we need every day. God is the only one who can help us. (Maria)

For Maria, the structural violence of urban poverty is unendurable without God, who provides a wealth of spirit that fills the place of, and is superior to, material wealth. The Catholic Church, as an intermediary with God, provides an institutional link between material suffering and moral salvation. Interestingly, the wickedness and corruption that Maria identifies is not just a limited perception of the barrio's, or even the nation's, moral condition. During my visits to La Ciénaga over the years, both Pentecostals and Catholics pointed to national disasters around the globe, including Hurricane Katrina (2005), the Chilean earthquakes (2005 and 2007), and the Haitian earthquake (2010), as evidence that the end is indeed nigh. People seek solace in religion's conservative morality as an antidote to the "corruption" that characterizes the "end of times."

The upshot of this emphasis on a global moral crisis is that it diverts attention from the structural causes of poverty and attempts to create a more equal world. When individual wickedness is blamed for the world's problems, and the destruction of the world is presented as the only viable solution, it should not be surprising that few residents believe in political pathways. Pentecostal congregations are not encouraged to be optimistic about the material world, and Catholic congregations espouse mixed messages, varying between viewing material change as possible and explaining inequalities as God's will. Indeed, I observed that the laity tended to be more likely to attribute poverty to God than were the Jesuit priests, who put in significant effort to educate the congregation about the causes of poverty. The laity's insistence on poverty as a divine condition made it difficult for the Jesuits to mobilize residents politically. As a result, the core group of community activists consisted of a few dozen people out of a barrio of eighteen thousand residents. However, this does not mean that religious practice in La Ciénaga is not political. The public nature of religious practice in the barrio, combined with the barrio's pressing material needs, makes religious practice a political statement regardless of intent. In fact, the Catholic Church's ability to amass large groups of participants to its events is perhaps the best indicator of its power as a connector between citizens and political vehicles such as the state.

WHEN FAITH BECOMES POLITICS

At three o'clock in the afternoon on Sunday January 30, 2005, three large coaches transported cienigüeros to the city's Olympic Stadium for a large Catholic rally. There were around ten thousand people in attendance from various barrios around the city, seated according to their community groups and wearing clothes in their community's colors. Many waved flags bearing the national emblem, or images of the island of Hispaniola with the words *República Dominicana* printed on them. The color of the parish San Martín de Porres (combining La Ciénaga and Guachupita) is white, which is also the color of the PRD. This prompted Maria to joke with Adela that people might mistake the group for lost PRD supporters who had turned up for a political rally eight months late. Most of the attendees from La Ciénaga were women, reflecting their dominance in the Catholic Church's congregation. At one end of the stadium was a stage decorated with a backdrop of painted makeshift icons of the Mother Mary, the infant Jesus, and the twelve disciples. An altar, flowers, and various crosses were positioned on the stage. To the left hung a banner reading "We want a peaceful Dominican Republic."

As the rally began, a group of priests entered the stadium and proceeded across the field to the stage amidst the cheering and clapping of participants. The opening speech set the agenda: the launching of the Third Pastoral Plan, a blueprint for the organization of the church's activities in Santo Domingo. The church presented the plan as a joint project between the church and the barrios to constitute and expand a world community of Catholics, who would work together globally to spread Christianity and end poverty.

The women of La Ciénaga enjoyed themselves immensely that afternoon: they were proud of the number of people present, representing many barrios; they admired the beauty of the priests' vestments; they enthusiastically joined in the singing of religious songs, and reflected on the speeches. Perhaps most importantly, they appreciated their inclusion in a phenomenon that extended far beyond their barrio, linking them with Catholics from across Santo Domingo to imagine a moral and spiritual project that encompasses the entire world. For people like Adela and Maria, the Catholic Church is the only institution that has ever invited them to participate in social life on such a broad scale. In fact, the two women rarely leave the barrio or its immediate surroundings except to attend church excursions to rallies, picnics, and Jesuit graduations. These days, the church is literally their only ticket out of Santo Domingo.

State celebrations have rather a different aesthetic to Catholic ones, although they are just as entertaining. On February 27, almost one month after the Catholic rally, **capitaleños** (residents of the capital city) lined Santo Domingo's **malecón** (waterfront) to watch the Independence Day parade marking the Dominican Republic's separation from Haiti in 1844. Attendees cheerfully jostled for position in the early afternoon to witness the passing of their nation's military, who were dressed in a colorful array of uniforms, hats, and emblems. Among the floats rolling by were the tanks of the Comando Especial Contra Terrorismo (Special Anti-Terrorist Command), bearing black-uniformed men with red berets, painted faces, and M16 rifles; a white-jacketed brass marching band; and ground soldiers in camouflage gear. The parade's high point involved paratroopers gliding down from planes to land on a stage. It was a performance of how the Dominican state would like to be seen by its citizenry and other nations: modern, progressive, and vigilant in the face of real and anticipated threats to sovereignty and order. And yet the parade's militarism, largely taken for granted, also spoke of self-conscious state power ready to act, even against its own citizens. Military power, the parade implied, was part of progress.

Close by, most cienigüeros did not venture out from under the bridge to view the parade. Many watched it on their television sets—a feat made possible by the unexpected provision of electricity all evening, possibly a favor granted by the state and the private electricity company to allow barrio residents to witness this spectacle of state prowess. In fact, that day *la luz* (the light) did not go off again until four the following morning, inspiring much revelry and happiness in La Ciénaga, and inciting Adela to comment to me that "they must have forgotten to turn it off." The existence of such favors suggests that, despite the state's increasing involvement in the barrio, cienigüeros still feel abandoned. Instead, the Catholic Church is viewed as the barrio's primary supporter. In Adela's words, "Everything good that has been done in La Ciénaga has had to do with the priests. They have moved us forward. Without the priests we are nothing."

Cienigüeros view the church as their primary provider despite the fact that the state, not the church, is the most significant institutional force in their lives. National identity cards, voting in elections, provision of schooling, health clinics, and hospitals, subsidized food, subsidized medicine, wage protection, transport, and utilities are just some of the goods and services that the state provides. Catholicism tends to obscure the state's contributions because the church is so directly implicated in people's daily lives. Furthermore, the church has political power through its strong relationship with the state and its status as a powerful global institution. As Felix explained to me:

> The Church, particularly the Catholic Church, we know it has a lot of power. When the Catholic Church pronounces that it is in favor of or against something, generally the government pays attention because although the government represents a great power, the Catholic Church has a universal power.

Organized religion is particularly relevant in Santo Domingo's barrios due to their lack of trust in political mechanisms. While residents can vote for their government representatives, politics is widely viewed as corrupt, benefiting the elites but rarely the poor (see Ferguson 1992). It is commonly believed that one does not go into politics to help one's community, but for personal gain. Ferguson points out that the belief that politicians are corrupt is so entrenched that Dominicans say that people who go into politics are looking for "una botella" (a bottle). This term refers to the appearance of a particular government building, located in Gazcue, that resembles a crate of bottles. If you work in the crate, so it is thought, you can—and will—appropriate bottles for yourself. Even a person with honorable intentions will be seduced by the opportunity to *sacar beneficios* (take benefits) upon entering politics or any other position of power. Felix and others lamented to me that the few cienigüeros who have been elected to municipal office won their positions because they promised to help barrio residents, but they turned their backs on the community as soon as they were elected. This lack of faith in politicians—the belief that absolute power corrupts absolutely—is widespread among Dominicans both inside and outside the barrio, and affects the ways in which they engage politically. Unable to trust political processes, and with few avenues to enact direct and meaningful change, many cienigüeros act to improve their own lives or the futures of their family members, rather than working toward—or even believing in—a politics that could transform the community or the nation.

The little political action that does take place among citizens tends to be short-lived. A telling example of the fleeting nature of political action was a brief revolt in 1984 against an agreement between the Dominican government and the **IMF**. This agreement imposed a program of austerity on the Dominican Republic with the aim of addressing an external debt of US$2.4 billion (Ferguson 1993; Sagás 2000). The IMF program caused a steep rise in the cost of living, with the price of pharmaceuticals increasing by 200 percent and a range of staples by 100 percent (Ferguson 1993, 566). The peso, previously tied to the U.S. dollar, was devalued, and wages were cut. On April 23, 1984, a twelve-hour strike and riots left 112 people dead (most shot by security forces), 500 wounded, and 5,000 arrested (Ferguson 1993, 566). The riots destroyed the last remnants of the PRD government's popularity and brought the economic problems of the Dominican Republic to the world's attention. Middle-class groups, consisting mainly of service professionals, also began to agitate for better conditions. A number of popular organizations grew out of the 1984 revolt, including *Comités de la Lucha Popular* (Popular Struggle Committees), which were established in an attempt to coordinate different forms of national action. However, these organizations failed to take hold in any significant way (Ferguson 1993).

Conversely, the Catholic Church has been a major player in the Dominican political scene for decades, if not centuries. Trujillo's dictatorship depended on church support and use of religious symbolism. It permitted the church to pursue its ecclesiastical activities so long as they did not interfere in the state's economic and ideological programs (Betances 2007; Derby 2009). However, toward the end of Trujillo's reign, the church eventually denounced the regime's violence publicly. During the political turbulence of the 1960s and 1970s, the Catholic

Church reframed its politics around ideas of liberal democracy and social change. It took on a central role as mediator of political disputes, such as accusations of electoral fraud (Sáez 2007). It also presented itself as a leader in the transition from authoritarian rule to liberal democracy, advising on legislation, founding civil organizations, and campaigning for services and development in poor communities. It is not the only religious organization that provides tangible benefits to its congregation, nor did it necessarily lead the way. From the 1940s onward, forms of Pentecostalism that offered their congregations faith healing and greater levels of participation contributed to the growth of evangelical churches. Since Vatican II (1962–1965), the Catholic Church in Latin America embraced liberation theology, which teaches social justice with reference to modern notions of emancipation (Vásquez 1999). They instituted the "preferential option for the poor," redistributing some forms of power and control to the laity and combining spiritual teaching with political practice (Vallier 1971). The Catholic Church's increased focus on providing social goods is therefore just as much an outcome of a need to compete in an increasingly pluralistic, *global*, religious marketplace as it is a response to conditions in the Dominican Republic.

Whereas any conflict of interest between the Dominican state and the Catholic Church was muted during authoritarian rule, today the church's ideological and material projects frequently diverge from those of the state (Vallier 1971). The Catholic Church's breadth of influence renders it capable of being a significant force for affecting social change. Its embeddedness in local communities, strong state relations, and status as a global institution gives it an advantage over other religious, political, and economic organizations. Depending on local context, the church may work directly in poor communities to provide services (such as education, health, and political training), campaign for the state to install services, promote legislative changes, or help poor communities seek resources from other sources (such as international NGOs) (see Levine 1992; Shepherd 1993). While the church works with the state on many occasions to coordinate its social programs, in other instances it bypasses the state altogether in favor of working directly with communities or with international organizations.

However, despite its significant autonomy, the Catholic Church's involvement in politics and social change is ultimately dependent on

relations with their host state's institutions and its incumbent government. When state and church interests conflict (such as during Trujillo's dictatorship), the state tends to reduce the church's role in politics
and welfare, such as through limiting the church's role in education or
evicting priests it considers to be acting against the state's interest.
Conversely, when state and church interests align, the church may be
more politically conservative and less critical of its host government.
The church's own division of labor permits the management of these
divergent interests. Higher-ranking church officials tend to take a conservative political position, while the Jesuits administer poverty-reduc-
tion programs and actively critique the state. This internal division of
labor assists the church in appearing to serve the state's and civilians'
best interests, regardless of whether they are aligned or in conflict.

THE OPTION FOR THE POOR IN LA CIÉNAGA

Santo Domingo's barrios were some of the early beneficiaries of the
Catholic Church's shift toward the "preferential option for the poor."
The Jesuits, led by the priest and anthropologist Jorge Cela, founded
Centro Bonó in 1993 to undertake social-justice research and support
political organization in the barrios. They train Jesuit students, conduct
social research, run community leadership courses for barrio residents,
hold conferences, and provide a refugee service for Haitian immigrants.
Centro Bonó relies on funding from international aid agencies, consul-
tancies for other institutions, the sale of publications, and donations. It
also houses the CES (Centro de Estudios Sociales Padre Juan Montalvo), which edits the academic journal *Estudios Sociales*. The center's
staff and academics conduct research on urban poverty, prepare reports
and press releases on social issues, and coordinate development projects in a number of poor neighborhoods in the National District and in
Boca Chica (a resort town located half an hour's drive east of Santo
Domingo). The stated aim of the CES is not to undertake development
projects itself, but to train community leaders to campaign for funding
and coordinate the implementation of development projects.

The church's presence in the barrios was not initiated spontaneous-
ly, but emerged during conflicts between the barrios and the Dominican state. In 1977, the COPADEBA was founded with the assistance of

the church in response to widespread barrio evictions (see Ferguson 1992). Its aim was to coordinate activities among the poor barrios to campaign for their fair treatment and land rights. This organization was still active during my 2009 visit. La Ciénaga's elected representative would attend regular meetings of the COPADEBA and also meetings of La Ciénaga's own coordinating body, the Ciénaga Cooperative for Development (CODECI), thus serving as a link between the groups.

CODECI was founded in La Ciénaga in 1988 following the destruction wrought by Hurricane George. CODECI holds public meeting once every two weeks, and organizational meetings every other week, in its office in La Clarín. The public meetings are attended by representatives from most of the barrio's community organizations. Representatives use the forum to report on their activities, request assistance, and discuss the barrio's problems. Representatives of organizations from outside La Ciénaga may also attend these meetings to discuss projects planned for the barrio. The CES founded the group, prepared its constitution, and provides ongoing funding, oversight, and training to community leaders, including offering a diploma in community leadership. During my residency, a number of CODECI officers undertook this diploma.

While the Catholic Church dominates political organization in La Ciénaga, other churches have also been known to get involved. During the evictions of 1991, other churches also mobilized to support residents:

> When the evictions of 1991 occurred the churches understood that their role wasn't only to pray or preach about God, but that they were also encumbered with a responsibility and that was to defend the rights of the parishioners and the people in a general sense. All these churches understood that they should unite forces, and it was the first time that I ever saw Evangelists, Jehovah's Witnesses, and Catholics get together in favor of a cause, to defend the rights of every single one of the people who were going to be evicted.
>
> I remember that all the churches got together and agreed on this. They understood that their role wasn't just to pray, because Jesus Christ came to the world and he didn't only pass his time praying but he also passed it doing a series of works in favor of the people. If they follow Jesus Christ too, they should emulate his actions to serve the people, to help them resolve their problems. (Felix)

In Felix' s understanding, the churches put aside their rivalries to create a unified front as Christians, inspired by the actions of Christ to help the poor. Pentecostal churches support other social initiatives, including a kindergarten. However, these direct actions are rare. Organizations founded by the Catholic Church, especially the CES, COPADEBA, and CODECI, remain the primary institutions for community development. Yet even the imaginaries of the residents who work with these organizations can be clouded by a discourse that presents La Ciénaga and its people as a moral failure. Cienigüeros do not just lack faith in the political system or capitalism; they also lack faith in each other. The Catholic Church's position of power should therefore be understood in terms of its monopoly over trust, as well as its command of material and spiritual resources.

IMAGINING THE FUTURE

On a shelf in the CES's library sits a book outlining a grand plan for the future of La Ciénaga and the neighboring barrio of Los Guandules. The plan's numerous colored maps promise a remarkable transformation from the barrio's current state into an orderly and spacious urban suburb. Gone are the ramshackle houses sinking into the swamp in the low-lying lands, replaced instead by parks and baseball pitches. While the older core of housing, built on a rocky hill, has been retained in the plan, the dwellings that are currently perched precariously next to the polluted Ozama River have been replaced by a park and walkway that spans the bank for the entire length of the barrio. New services, such as a medical center and a kindergarten, occupy corners where colmados once existed, and wider thoroughfares allow city buses to collect passengers. The entire effect is of a modest but pleasant waterside suburb that is a far cry from the muddy "nest of crabs" that characterized the barrio in the 1970s. La Ciénaga, the swamp, has been gentrified in this work of fiction.

This idyllic vision comes from Plan Cigua (Navarro 2004), which was developed by an organization called Ciudad Alternativa (Alternative City). It builds on, and reinforces, the hope that is held by the community's leaders that La Ciénaga's future will be a better one, both materially and morally. It is one of a number of attempts to systematize the development of the barrio. In 2004 the CES and the Catholic Organization for Relief and Development (CORDAID) produced a booklet called the Agenda for Work for Barrio Development for La Ciénaga. The agenda details La Ciénaga's demography, the infrastructure problems of the barrio, and the actions taken by various local and external organizations working for its development.

Generally speaking, these development plans are not particularly contested. They recommend relocating residents currently living in the dangerous and inconvenient parts of the barrio to alternative sites around Santo Domingo. If carried out fairly, with adequate housing provided, I suspect it is likely that most residents would consider the relocations to be reasonable and even welcome. In recent years, there have been a handful of small, successful relocations that have been broadly accepted and provide an early indication that barrio redevelopment can in fact be successful. However, cienigüeros do not necessarily agree on how development should take place, who the beneficiaries should be, or whether it is actually possible for these plans to come to fruition. Gabriel, the leader of a sports-education club and a CODECI representative, describes his hopes for the barrio's future using economy and nature as metaphors, arguing, "We want to *llevar mas adelante* (take ourselves forward). As they say, a diamond is made of carbon, but once you polish it, it shines. That is, you bring out the value. As an institution we could prepare a fertile terrain; that is, the seed that we plant today will turn the barrio into fertile terrain for development." In Gabriel's view, the barrio and its people have an intrinsic value that can be coaxed into revealing itself. Such a possibility requires craftsmanship and nurturing, rather than violence and struggle. Gabriel's dream is emblematic of how cienigüeros would *prefer* to move **pa'lante** (forward) if conditions were favorable: to transcend the "violences of everyday life" (Scheper-Hughes 1992) through a process that balances social and economic concerns.

Not all community leaders' views are quite so hopeful or inclusive. For the leader of one of La Ciénaga's neighborhood councils, Orlando, the barrio is redeemable, but many residents lack the intelligence necessary to understand the problems that the barrio faces:

> I think that for the future—this is speculation, like dreaming—but I
> think that within a short time it will be necessary to evict the people

who live in the uninhabitable zone at the edge of the Ozama River. They live in extreme danger. We understand, although one can't say it to them because they don't understand. Their abilities don't permit them to understand that they live in danger. I believe that for the future we should evict this group of people because they live so close to the river that their backyard is water. Here where we live, where you live, where I live in Clarín, I believe with time this could urbanize, and so that a large portion of La Ciénaga could live in this sector in high buildings.

Such a redevelopment should entail building new housing for the evicted, though the design and realization of this process is largely left to the government. Yet Orlando's statement does not acknowledge that many residents currently live in dangerous locations because they have nowhere else to go. It took a natural disaster to force the government to relocate residents living on the most unstable parts of the cliffs separating La Ciénaga from the city. On August 28, 2008, eight people died in neighboring Guachupita (on the cliff above La Ciénaga) when a landslide caused by Tropical Storm Gustav buried their houses. The Catholic Church led a mass protest and the resulting media pressure caused the government to announce a program to relocate 150 families from the area to a new settlement located near Herrera Airport on the city's western edge. This new settlement is slightly closer to the city than Las Caobas, where some residents were relocated in 1977. The program provided the relocated families with housing and furniture, a small plot of farmland for each household, and agricultural training. The beneficiaries were required to contribute a certain quota of labor to build their new homes. The project was finally finished in 2011 and the families were moved. It struck me as somewhat strange that the state expected fully urbanized families to "return" to a rural lifestyle, but given that the site is within the city's periphery, the families have retained urban access. The city's west is not the isolated periphery that it was back in 1977 during the first relocations, and the new residences are within two kilometers of a new metro line that opened on April 1, 2013. One of Adela's sons, Eduardo, was among the people who were relocated. He continues to work in his stable security job in the city during the night, and plants vegetables in his garden in his spare time. Having been born in the city, he has approached his newly gained land with a great deal of curiosity and interest. His youngest son, Jeffrey, moved in with Adela when Eduardo relocated in order to finished high school nearby and undertake technical training in refrigeration. Jeffrey visits his father on the weekends and helps him research farming methods in library books.

Whereas Orlando and Eduardo feel that it is possible to improve the barrio by resolving some of its more pressing problems, other residents feel that it would be better for the barrio to be abandoned altogether. Angelo, whose conversion to Pentecostalism I mentioned earlier in this chapter, moved to Santo Domingo from another town and settled in La Ciénaga on the recommendation of a friend. He chose the barrio because it is close to the city center and is inexpensive to live in. Angelo runs a carpentry workshop and employs two young, local men as his assistants. But despite seeming fairly settled and successful in La Ciénaga, he upholds a decidedly negative view of the barrio:

> Well, I think that the first thing that should be done is a total eviction where the people who live in this sector can have a place to live better, somewhere that is within reach of everything, where people can go quickly to the doctor, where they can easily go to a school, and convert this area into either a tourist zone or military zone. In this way some of the city's delinquency could be eliminated.

In other words, Angelo considers the entire barrio to be unredeemable. His opinion goes beyond a simple assessment of the material conditions of the barrio and whether they are fit for human habitation. Rather, he associates the barrio's material poverty with a problem of moral failure in which the barrio is an incubator for crime. The material and the moral, in this rendering, are inseparable. Just as the world is morally corrupt and can only be saved by its destruction in the apocalypse, so is the barrio a prime candidate for demolition.

The rejection of the possibility of material transformation, whether through old-fashioned class action or neoliberal salvation, entails quite different aspirations for the future than the idea of material transformation. The end of the world presents worldly change as inconsequential in light of the coming apocalypse. Yet the fact that both development and apocalypse are communicated and practiced through material mediums suggests that people do not see any contradiction in objectifying aspirations that are meant to transcend physical form. Hence, whether we are discussing the development of a poor barrio, or a reliance on religion to cope with difficult lives, materiality is the medium through which lives are lived and changes implemented.

This materiality is not concerned simply with creating or rejecting wealth. Rather, the practice of religion through material forms has both economic and moral aspects. For some individuals, poverty bestows moral superiority; for others, poverty indicates moral failure. Residents make judgments about whether the community can truly transform based on their assessment of the collective wickedness of residents, the nation, and the entire world. In the following chapter I describe how this moral discourse has developed in relation to economic crisis and a subsequent rise in crime.

5

MOVING PLACES

Barrios as Barometers of National Progress

In 2004, the PLD's Presidential candidate, Leonel Fernandez, campaigned for the upcoming election with the slogan *¡E'pa'lante que vamos!* a colloquial abbreviation of the longer *¡Es para adelante que vamos!* or "It's forward we go!" The campaign proved successful, ushering Fernandez into his second (nonconsecutive) term as president with a clear majority. Fernandez's slogan held a dual appeal for Dominicans: it built upon an existing egalitarian discourse of national progress and it promised a break from the economic atrophy experienced under the previous president, the PRD's Rafael Hipólito Mejía, whose policies resulted in rocketing inflation and unemployment.

During the presidential campaign, the intended spirit of the political slogan was illustrated on the president's website (www.epalantequevamos.com). An entry page played upbeat techno music, while banners with images and words moved across the page, advertising the campaign's themes: the word *dignity* overlaid on a photo of Fernandez with the Pope; *education* showing a dark-skinned child wearing a school uniform and using a computer; *health* with an image inside a hospital ward; *work* showing scientists busy in a lab, and *development* on a photo of a busy road with an overpass.

After this introduction, the homepage showed a welcome message and a prominent color cartoon depicting a jubilant man who has just finished crossing a bridge. He is a typical Dominican character: masculine, mustached, light-skinned yet not quite white, and dressed in working clothes, boots, and a cap. The scene behind him, on the side of the bridge he has just left, is reminiscent of Halloween, with thunder and lightning, darkness and bats, and an alligator baring its teeth. It is labeled *chaos*. The bridge is labeled *100 days* in reference to celebrations for Leonel's first hundred days in his second term as president. The scene that the man is entering is full of light from the rising sun, grass, and flowers. He has three paths in front of him: *order* to his left, *confidence* in front, and *stability* to his right. He holds his hands in the air and his face is lifted up toward the sky as he exclaims, "¡E'pa'lante que vamos!" By depicting the man as having arrived at the other side of the bridge, the cartoon illustrates the government's main argument: despite repeated setbacks in the past, the nation has already begun its journey back on the road of progress in a mere one hundred days of rational governance.

During my main fieldwork in 2005, the slogan "¡E'pa'lante que vamos!" became a catch phrase in La Ciénaga. Cries of "It's forward we go!" would resonate regularly in community meetings and prayer groups. At first it was evoked seriously, reflecting residents' optimism in their new government. But eventually, as residents' initial enthusiasm for the new government waned, its use became more ironic than inspirational, and it would be brought out on the most inappropriate (and amusing) of occasions.

Ambivalence over the president's slogan was not limited to the barrios. Throughout the nation, a restless worry permeated residents' sense of security. Social and economic changes since the 1980s had propelled rising crime rates. The association between economic crisis and crime further cemented already-negative views of urban poverty that have their roots in the late nineteenth century. Within this enhanced climate of insecurity, barrios designated as *abajo el puente* (under the bridge) have become more than localized development problems: they are viewed as an obstacle to achieving the kind of progress that Dominican elites have dreamed about since at least the time of Juan Pablo Duarte, one of the nation's founding fathers, and after whom one of the bridges spanning the Ozama River is named.

The Dominican Republic's dreams of progress have material manifestations of various kinds. Economically, they inspired the planning and redevelopment of the capital city, with the construction of wide boulevards, bridges, national monuments, and a geometric aesthetics in residential areas and public spaces. They also fueled ideas about moral order, including the effects of urban life on human behavior and the institutionalization of the national racial archetype, the indio.

History and ideology are objectified in all of these material things, people, and places. However, this is not to say that their meanings are fixed and unchanging. In fact, as our man crossing the bridge indicates, an important part of progress is social and economic change. Metaphors of movement are used in the Dominican Republic to indicate progress as well as to talk about circulation in the economy. For example, the phrase *"no hay movimiento en la* **calle***"* (there is no movement in the street) is uttered to indicate that the economy is moving slowly (figure 5.1). Alternatively, if a Dominican tells you that there were "many people drinking and dancing" at a festival, they are often implying that there was also a lot of money changing hands. In other words, the movement of money, goods, and people is positive and necessary because it fuels growth.

There is, however, a catch. Too much movement, or the wrong kinds of movement by the wrong kinds of people, can also signal moral failure. According to popular wisdom, drinking and dancing may be signs of a happy and prosperous population, but they threaten to degenerate into disorder, irresponsible spending, and even crime, as less wealthy people are seduced by the good life and give up their moral values in order to keep up with their wealthier neighbors. In this chapter I discuss how Santo Domingo's barrios have become a kind of moral barometer of national well-being or failure. Specifically, there are two kinds of mobility that the poor engage in that are considered a threat to progress: their migration from the countryside to the city (due to the innate corrupting powers of the barrios), and the movement of thieves from the barrios into the city to steal (because they will not rob in their own neighborhoods). While much discussion of the barrios' immorality in the media and among the public focuses on crime in relation to mobility, I show how these stigmas are largely inspired by the barrios' visible poverty, not by actual crime rates. Unpacking the materiality of the barrios' criminalization, and residents' responses, can help us to understand the fears and hopes of Dominicans and their orientations toward the future.

Figure 5.1. Street life is an integral part of the "movement" that drives urban economies. *Photograph courtesy of the author.*

METAPHORS OF MOVEMENT, IMAGINARIES OF PLACE

Movement has long been an important metaphor and a contentious issue in the Dominican Republic. Writing about the importance of ***movimiento*** (movement) for Dominicans living in the town of Andrés, next to the tourist enclave of Boca Chica, Gregory argues:

> Movement here is not merely a metaphor for earning a living: it is precisely this movement—whether across the policed landscape of the ***zona turística***, or the frontiers of the export manufacturing enclaves, or the international division of labor—that has been the target of neoliberal strategies of accumulation. As capital has become increasingly mobile . . . labor has become ever more shackled to space—space that has been increasingly disciplined and privatized. (Gregory 2007, 239)

Residents of Andrés have daily contact with global flows through their work in tourism and export manufacturing, but they have little chance to achieve for themselves the mobility of others that they witness. Instead, they are incorporated asymmetrically into a "spatial economy of difference," that is, a hierarchy of color, class, and moral worth that is associated with particular geographic spaces. The spatial economy of difference protects privilege and facilitates the reinforcement of hierarchy on a daily basis.

Gregory's study is a much-needed counterbalance to the vast literature on Dominican international migration (see Grasmuck and Pessar 1991; Vicioso 2000), which far outweighs studies of Dominicans at home. While an important object of investigation, this profusion of interest in "dominicanyork" and other transnational identities overlooks the fact that the majority of Dominicans cannot migrate due to the unfavorable position of the Dominican Republic in the global economy, and of the nation in the global moral order. Even if the residents of Andrés were to save enough money from their meager wages to buy a ticket to the United States, they would stand little chance of gaining even a visitor's visa due to their lack of plausible securities. For the residents of Andrés, movimiento does not signify international migration but rather their limited chances of economic and social mobility within their local communities. Their localization testifies to the power of the transnational economy.

Unlike Gregory's study, the residents of La Ciénaga (located half an hour's drive west of Andrés) do not make a living in global industries such as tourism or factory work. Instead, they work overwhelmingly in the city's service industry as domestic servants, security guards, construction workers, and street vendors. However, their experiences of both globalization and localization are similar. Cienigüeros migrate from the country to the city in search of a modern life and possibilities for progress, but the vast majority find that the barrios act as a terminus for their aspirations. Despite a profusion of international links, remittances, migration experience, and relatives abroad, progress beyond the barrio is difficult. Barrio residents find themselves "shackled to space" by virtue of their position in the lowest stratum of those who nonetheless depend on a global economy.

Poor Dominicans who aspire to progress encounter multiple obstacles in their path. The first of these obstacles is the dilemma of whether

to move to the city, often a hostile environment for the poor. Historically, migration of all kinds has been regarded with a skeptical eye by elites
and the general public alike. In the social imaginaries of the Dominican
Republic, *el campo* (the countryside) is cast as the heartland of Dominican national character and represents an idyllic past, whereas the city is
the site for citizenship and the production of the nation's modern future
(Derby 1998; Martínez-Vergne 2005). Dominican social history has
been dominated by peasant production, and rural people have long
been seen as major players in the development of Dominican culture.
El campo was the setting of important events in Dominican history,
such as the 1844 War of Independence against Haiti, the birth of national leaders, and the development of folklore (Andrade 1969; Sagás
2000; Torres-Saillant 1998). A romanticized rendering of el campo
dominates representations of Dominican culture in written history,
painting, and music. Martínez-Vergne writes how at the beginning of
the nineteenth century, the "composite ideal Dominican was based in
the countryside" (2005, 21) and included characteristics like color
(more white than black), affinity with Europe (as opposed to the United
States), and love of country (hard work, family, and morality). The
large, central valley known as Cibao is particularly associated with these
characteristics, because its fertility made it a popular settlement site for
European immigrants. Today, relations with the United States have
eclipsed ties with Europe, but notions of the authentic Dominican archetypal character continue to be based on these early imaginings of el
campo. Country people, particularly those with lighter skin, are given a
privileged place in national imaginings as carriers of culture and morality (Taylor 2009a).

Dependence on agricultural production and late industrialization
meant that Dominican cities remained small until the 1960s. As a result,
many city dwellers of all social classes are first- or second-generation
migrants who retain respect for rural life and strong connections with
their relatives in the countryside. While el campo is seen as backward
compared with the city, it is imagined as a place that is largely uncor-
rupted by negative aspects of modern urban living, such as disease and
crime. Unlike tourists, who flock to the nation's beaches, Dominicans
take advantage of public holidays to head inland to visit relatives and
bathe in freshwater rivers. City residents visit the country to visit family

and escape the ills of city living, such as pollution, noise, overcrowding, disease, stress, and crime.

Residents of La Ciénaga remember rural life with nostalgia. Compared to present struggles to maintain employment and buy expensive imported foods, the rural past is perceived to have been a time of abundance and social equality. Hard work and good social relations ensured that everyone had their share:

> Country life is different and I'm going to tell you why. Country life is rich, very good, firstly because you breathe clean air; secondly because there is less licentiousness, less delinquency, and a more favorable environment in which to subsist. Such as the heat, there is less heat, the river is rich, very good, the food is vegetables, sugar cane, fruits, and is much better because we cultivate it. If I don't have something, someone will give it to me.
>
> But life in the country is also more difficult. If you start a business selling food in a shop, people want to buy on credit and it's hard to get them to pay because there aren't many means of production because businesses have a small profit margin and so they don't pay very good wages. But money goes farther in the country because there is less to spend it on. Here in the city, if you go out to the street to sell coffee, eggs, cigarettes, mangoes, avocados, and food, you will sell it. (Diego)

In Diego's assessment, the countryside, which represents health and morality, competes with economic production and mass consumption in the city. Reflecting on rural life helps migrants like Diego to evaluate modern urban life. The city has not met his expectations of economic advancement, and in crucial ways falls short of the social life of the countryside, but it offers choices that are not available in the country due to a deficit of economic production. Unless one has enough money to shorten the experiential distance between rural and urban life, city life offers a greater range of opportunities for the poor to engage with modernity. The poor may remember el campo nostalgically, but they also remember what they came to the city to find, and what they have been denied. Much of the idyllic reminiscing about the country is a response to the adverse conditions of urban poverty rather than a wish to return to a rural past. Migrants speak of relocating to the country only if they can do so on middle-class terms, that is, with enough money to live comfortably.

One problem that migrants to Santo Domingo's barrios face is that they risk losing their status as the respectable poor. One street vendor, Juan, claimed that " they're the barrios where the *tígueres* (tigers) are, people who come from the country for the capital. Those who stay in the city are these *delincuentes* (delinquents), no-one else." In other words, if barrio residents were moral people, they would never have migrated from the countryside—or, upon arriving, they would have recognized the evil of the barrios and immediately returned to where they came from. This view is sometimes upheld by aspiring migrants to the barrios. Around half of Felix's family have migrated to Santo Domingo over the past few decades, but not all have stayed. One of his uncles brought his wife and their child to La Ciénaga in order to put the child into a "good" school. However, they lasted approximately two weeks before they returned to Cibao. They were unnerved by gunshots being fired into the air and stories of robberies, and decided that they would be better off living a simple life with fewer chances of progress than risking their child's safety in the city. However, the perceived greater morality of the countryside rarely wins out: many more people are willing to take a risk in the city in the hope of achieving the kind of progress that President Fernandez promised.

BARRIO FEARS: WHERE IMMORALITY RESIDES

Throughout the 1990s and 2000s, the stigmatization of the barrios was compounded by a rising crime rate in urban centers and an increasing tendency to point to the barrios as the cause of the problem. The journalist Ruiz Matuk reported on July 17, 2005, that there were around 1,259 homicides by civilians in the Dominican Republic during first five months of 2005, representing an increase of 60 percent over the preceding decade. Many capitaleños swore to me that ten years previously there was no crime at all. During Trujillo's dictatorship and Balaguer's heavy-handed rule, the state monopolized violence and problems between citizens were relatively rare. When crime rates began to rise, capitaleños became disturbed not only because they felt they faced greater danger, but also because they felt that the national character was changing. The image of the Dominican as friendly and sociable, mixing with neighbors on the street, was threatened as people retreated behind locked and barred doors. One newspaper report suggested that the growing fear of crime was not necessarily related to an overall *increase* in crime, but to a feeling that crime was spilling out of the barrios and into middle-class areas. An article in the Santo Domingo newspaper *Listín Diario* complained:

> In the leafy suburb of Gazcue, the residents cannot sleep in peace. The fear of being assaulted at any time prevents them sleeping. The wave of robberies, assaults, and attacks, characteristic of almost all the popular [poor] barrios of the city of Santo Domingo, have arrived at this historic middle class area. (Pérez Reyes 2005)

Reyes presented the problem as one of transgression: criminal behavior is no longer contained in its site of origin but is manifest in a neighborhood that was previously safe. This is alarming because it represents social change and uncertainty (Taylor 2009b). Conversely, another journalist protested the measures that people have taken to protect themselves. In a newspaper article published on March 6, 2005, titled "Open the Doors," Gautreaux Piñeyro commented:

> Years ago, the majority of houses remained with their doors open and the danger of someone entering to rob the house was perhaps one in a thousand. Is there such a large economic bonanza that Dominicans have locked themselves up in their houses with bars, electronic alarm systems, motorized gates, and other modes of protection? Almost without noticing we have allowed ourselves to get cornered: robbery, assault, attacks, in one word, crime appears to have won the game over decent people, working people.

Whereas the first article diagnosed the illness, the second describes what the middle classes saw as a cure for themselves as individuals, if not for society. Crime has, shockingly, arrived in middle-class areas, and residents are reacting by hemming themselves into a corner. Interestingly, Gautreaux Piñeyro frames the problem as Dominicans having so much money that they can afford to take outlandish security measures. This contrasts with an alternative discourse that blames crime on economic crisis, but tellingly points to a widening gap between the wealthy and the poor. This greater economic distance propels the production of

a greater social distance in the form of a "moral panic" in which perceptions of danger, and responses to it, are disproportionate to actual risk
(Goode and Ben-Yehuda 1994):

> The point is, yes, fear and concern do, for the most part, grow out of
> the very real conditions of social life. But no, they need not be com-
> mensurate with the concrete threat posed specifically by that which
> is feared—indeed, that threat may not even exist in the first place. At
> the same time, concern is almost certainly based on some concretely
> real phenomenon—even though that which is feared, specifically,
> may be only tangentially related. (Goode and Ben-Yehuda 1994, 49)

Moral panic is produced through factors such as an increase in crime
rates, heightened media publicity, personal experiences, and a public
dialogue in which residents exchange rumors, personal experiences of
crime, eyewitness reports, and media reports. Through everyday talk,
consensus is reached on the nature and source of danger. As Caldeira
(2000) has noted in Brazil, the "talk of crime" is also a metaphor for
people to discuss other kinds of social ills. It "offers symbolism with
which to talk about other kinds of loss, such as downward mobility.
Moreover, crime adds drama to the narration of events that themselves
may be undramatic—for example, a forty-year process of change in a
neighborhood—but whose consequences can be distressing" (34).

In Santo Domingo, a widespread sense of instability feeds into a
"talk of crime" that particularly targets the poor barrios around the
Ozama River. Squatter settlements are considered to be potentially
dangerous spaces for everyone who enters them due to a combination
of threats including violence, crime, lack of sanitation, and underdevelopment. Furthermore, barrios are devoid of middle-class destinations
(such as shopping malls, universities, workplaces, and the homes of
family and friends) and nonresidents would have little cause to visit
them. The very first time I visited La Ciénaga, in January 2005, my taxi
driver was upset that I was making him drive into the barrio and warned
me that I would be "murdered for my shoes" if I visited the barrio.
When I told him that the Catholic Church had found me a place to live
there, he answered, "Then the Church is not your friend!" Residents of
these poor communities are isolated from the city's social life through
their lack of resources and geographic marginalization, evinced by the
reluctance of taxis to enter them.

The barrios are perceived to be not only dangerous to visit but also "dens of thieves" who prey on middle-class areas. As one capitaleño told me during a questionnaire I conducted in the city's center, "People are afraid of these sectors, it's the number-one theme. They [the delinquents] leave the barrios to steal things like cell phones." The view that the barrios are morally corrupt is compounded by attitudes that associate them with a racialized criminality. On at least three occasions after a robbery had taken place, I heard people (including the police) ask, "Was it a moreno?" when trying to gain a description of the perpetrator. While barrio residents represent a range of color shading, the average color is visibly darker in the poor barrios than in the wealthier parts of the city. The barrios are therefore associated with a racial profile (the moreno), a criminal profile (the delinquent), and a place (the barrio). These become conflated in the public's imagination, and as a result, one's physical appearance takes on a heightened importance in the city as people struggle to be perceived as respectable and achieve socioeconomic mobility.

In the Dominican Republic, contemporary beliefs about race and crime rest on a long history of state manipulation of scholarly research and public opinion concerning morality, race, and national identity (Derby 2003; Torres-Saillant 1998). National racism allocates moral disorder to dark-skinned people, especially "morenos" and "Haitianos." This fear of blackness stems from the Dominican Republic's long project to distance itself from its neighbor Haiti (perceived to be characterized by blackness, backwardness, poverty, and disorder) in favor of Europe and the United States (characterized by whiteness, progress, wealth, and civilization) (Torres-Saillant 1998). Unable to deny the African heritage of Dominican people, the dictator Trujillo invented the term *indio* in the 1930s. Today, *indio* is the paradigmatic descriptor of Dominican identity and is used by the state and civilians alike. Indeed, people who are classified in popular terms as "negro" or **blanco** are generally considered to be foreigners: the former are assumed to be Haitian, whereas blancos are American or European. Dark-skinned Dominicans are classified as "moreno" rather than "negro" to avoid denying them citizenship while simultaneously permitting an idiom of exclusion.

In contrast, whiteness signifies privilege and wealth. Lightening one's appearance, such as by bleaching one's skin or straightening one's hair, is commonly practiced to maximize chances in the job market and gain social acceptance as a person of value (see Candelario 2007). Maria, who is generally considered to be *indio claro* (light-skinned), told me about how, upon entering a store, the shopkeeper exclaimed, "Ah, a white woman! It's my lucky day!" Despite telling him that she lived in La Ciénaga, she could not convince him that she did not have much money to spend. In this particular case, light-colored skin trumped place of residence as a status symbol. However, this is not always the case: whether race trumps place depends on the context in which the judgment is taking place, and the values and identity of the people making the judgment.

While the term *indio* presents a solution to the polarizations of a white/black dualism, permitting the vast majority of Dominicans to claim a shared identity as part of *la raza dominicana* (the Dominican race), it feeds the talk of crime in two main ways. First, it perpetuates a myth of racial democracy and inclusion by representing blackness as something that does not exist in the Dominican Republic, hence denying that the talk of crime discriminates unfairly. Second, it delegitimizes an equal rights movement that has been successful elsewhere in the Caribbean in redressing racial discrimination, making the association of crime with race difficult to counteract. As a result, it is difficult to untangle the realities behind fears of crime. This has serious implications for protecting Dominicans from actual violence, whether they live inside or outside the barrios, and whether the source of crime is civilian or state.

PERCEPTIONS OF CRIME: MYTHS AND REALITIES

Although the "talk of crime" conflates a range of indicators of difference into one brand of criminalization, fears of the barrios are not solely based on prejudices. While I was living in La Ciénaga in 2005, it was not unusual to hear gunshots in the night, especially on weekends, as "tígueres tirando tiros" (tigers firing shots) argued about—I was repeatedly told—drugs and women. Spent bullets would be discovered on the streets in the mornings, numerous people reported being robbed, and one day a murdered lawyer washed up on the riverbank at the barrio's entrance. He was there when I passed by in the early morning, but the police did not turn up to investigate until late in the afternoon. In the meantime, it seemed like every single adult and child in the barrio found out who he was and went to see the dead body. Later, when I visited Santo Domingo's police headquarters to search data on crime in Santo Domingo, the inspector who helped me laughed at me for living in La Ciénaga. He showed me a murder map of the city, pointing out all the red dots representing murders in the barrio.

In a survey that I carried out in Santo Domingo's city center in 2005, my respondents considered La Ciénaga to be the fifth most dangerous barrio in the city. The other four barrios they identified (in order of danger, Capotillo, Guachupita, Gualey, and Los Guandules) are poor, medium-density barrios, three of which are also situated on the banks of the Ozama River. Curious about why these five barrios were chosen, I reviewed ten years of newspaper reports on crimes, from 1995 to 2005. Interestingly, I discovered that the media represent these five barrios in quite different ways. For example, most stories about La Ciénaga concern its poverty or perhaps instances of civil unrest. In contrast, most stories about the adjacent neighborhood, Guachupita, are about crime and gangs. However, my survey suggested that the general public does not particularly differentiate between the barrios: while they clearly rank some barrios as more dangerous than others, the "talk of crime" does not change much from one barrio to another.

Throughout the 1990s, most media coverage of La Ciénaga dealt with clashes between residents and the police rather than civilian crime. In 1995 the barrio had a run of bad press due to protests that took place inside the barrio between March and July of that year. Residents were protesting against the construction of a new sewage treatment plant in their barrio that was designed to receive waste from a neighboring suburb, not from La Ciénaga itself. The plant did not benefit La Ciénaga, whose waste continued to run into the river. On March 11, 1995, the newspaper *El Siglo* reported that protests of the day before had left two people dead (one young man shot by police and a woman from a reaction to tear gas) and dozens injured in clashes with the police (García 1995a). Protests continued for a few days until March 14, 1995, when the Balaguer government promised to relocate fifty families who lived immediately adjacent to the plant (García 1995b).

After Leonel Fernandez was inaugurated as president for the first time on August 16, 1996, the tone of media reports changed to focus on

La Ciénaga as a barrio that was characterized by abject poverty, but that was undergoing redevelopment. On September 4, 1996, *Hoy* quoted a document sent to the newspaper by a group of leaders from La Ciénaga that declares: "The barrio La Ciénaga has been converted into the sector with the worst physical and moral conditions, thanks to the arbitrary and unjust measures taken by the governments of the past twenty years" (Rámos 1996). Other articles published about La Ciénaga in 1996 included stories of overcrowding, disadvantaged children, public health, food distribution, the construction of housing, the ambiguity of land title, and, as the year draws to a close, youth gangs. The tone of these articles was increasingly one of injustice and the need for government action, rather than blaming the poor themselves. In 1997, Fernandez visited the barrio twice, in August and in December, to inaugurate the sewage treatment plant and mark the beginning of the construction of the school (*Nuevo Diario* 1997; Peña 1997).

In September 1998 residents of La Ciénaga formed CODECI. This organization took on the role of community public relations, and created dialogue with government institutions, and liaised with the media. From this time onward, there were fewer articles about La Ciénaga in the newspapers, and those that did appear generally referred to an ordered process of work and progress. By focusing on material improvements within the barrio, CODECI managed to influence the media to project an implicit message of a change in the moral order.

Guachupita is an interesting comparison to La Ciénaga because, although my survey respondents ranked it as the second most dangerous barrio in the city, it is frequently visited by outsiders. Guachupita borders the lively commercial district and is located at the top of the cliff that leads down to La Ciénaga and the Ozama River. It is a working-class suburb and its streets are laid out in a grid, lined with medium-density housing and three- or four-story, concrete apartment blocks. It also houses various schools and organizations. Guachupita is easier to access than La Ciénaga as it has plenty of public transport running through it. Despite its high level of development, Guachupita is noisy and has little of the community feel of La Ciénaga.

Guachupita began to figure strongly in the press in 1997. From this year onward, stories about Guachupita almost exclusively reported violence, public disorder, delinquency, and drugs. Particular attention was paid to gangs, gang violence, and gang culture, and the media exhibited none of the sympathy they show toward La Ciénaga. On October 1, 2004, *El Caribe* declared Guachupita to be in a "state of emergency" after a particularly noticeable week of gang activity in which two people died and nine were injured (Crousset 2004). The imagery and content of media reports of Guachupita were evocative of an inner-city, North American ghetto. Indeed, it is not unusual for Dominicans to blame return migrants for importing gang culture from the United States. By contrast, representations of La Ciénaga are more evocative of an urbanized World Vision advertising campaign, complete with images of naked children and substandard housing.

In some ways, newspaper stories about the barrios appeared more moderate than the stories I heard from people on the street. Overall, newspapers avoided blaming whole communities, reported police violence, published results from international investigations into human rights, and pointed to the structural causes of crime. Individuals, concerned with self-protection, were not as motivated to make this distinction. However, media focus on crime was almost certainly implicated in developing these negative public opinions in the first place. As Briceño-León and Zubillaga (2002) argue, fear "becomes uniform because the media make information on crime a daily occurrence, and the vicarious experience of victimization is emotionally stronger than the rational calculation of the risk" (30). Despite their different features and representations, the barrios were conflated in the public's imagination. Poverty and crime were both classified as sources of "danger," which became an overarching trope by which barrios and their residents were valued. Their place in the city's hierarchy was fixed through a blanket stigmatization.

CONTAINING VIOLENCE

If residents across the city and the media were united on one issue, it was that crime and violence needed to be contained. The wealthy and the poor alike called for an increase in police patrols in the barrios, saying, "The barrios need more police. When you go to a barrio they tell you, be careful!" In 2006, the Fernandez government extended a program called **Barrio Seguro** (Secure Barrio) to La Ciénaga. When I visited in July, groups of between four and six policemen were patrolling the barrio throughout the day and night. The program was widely publicized on the nightly television news, and a number of people I spoke with saw it as a force for good in the barrio. Pedro, a working-class resident of Villa Mella, in Santo Domingo's north, told me, "They [the barrios] are a bit more placated because there are many soldiers, more security, but there is delinquency. It's better than six months ago, a year ago."

Within the barrios, police efforts to reduce crime were met with a mixed reception. Many residents welcomed the police into the barrio. Since the launch of the Barrio Seguro program, residents have reported to me that La Ciénaga is much more tranquil than it was before, and the reduced number of gunshots at night indicates that they are correct. However, the police were (and arguably still are) perceived to be a significant part of the problem, as well as the solution. According to a Dominican newspaper, there were an estimated 1,376 extrajudicial as-sassinations by police in the Dominican Republic between 2000 and 2005 (Ramírez 2005). If these statistics are correct, the rate of extrajudi-cial assassinations by the police is around a quarter of the rate of civilian murders. In La Ciénaga, people fear their children are constantly in danger of being unfairly arrested, or worse. Stories of police corruption continue to abound, as Felix recounted to me in 2010:

> A lot of the police here are delinquents. You don't know who is going to do you damage, the police or the common delinquent. We have this terrible problem whereby we feel insecure walking down the street. It doesn't matter if the person at your side is dressed in a police uniform or in civil dress, young or old; you are afraid because you don't know if they are going to harm you.
>
> Last week a cousin of mine was arrested with his motorbike. When he was inside the station, a delinquent came along and he told the police officer in charge that he had stolen five gold chains. The officer said, "Where are the chains?" The delinquent said, "Look, here they are," and swapped them for the motorbike.
>
> I know of another case where a man was robbed of his motorbike and he went to the police station to report the person who did it. So the police officer called up the thieves to tell them that this person had reported them. The police are in league with the delinquents, and some of them are totally corrupt. (Felix)

The police are despised for using violence, yet violence is often tolerated when residents believe that "delinquents" are the victims. Miguel, a young, male neighbor of mine in La Ciénaga, lamented that the police don't kill enough delinquents. He said that Dominicans need "la mano dura" (a heavy hand) to keep them in order. In his view, Balaguer was justified in killing delinquents and dissidents because he at least kept the country calm. Although it is widely accepted in the Dominican Republic that the state and police are corrupt, criminal violence of the everyday variety is commonly perceived as a more immediate risk than the predations of the state. As a consequence, police abuses are tolerated.

The answer to this contradiction—of simultaneously supporting and condemning state abuse—lies in the ways in which Dominicans have historically viewed themselves in relation to the state. Centuries of caudillo politics, rebellion, dictatorships, and police violence have shaped Dominican thought regarding the efficacy of violence in controlling social disorder. Miguel's statement that Dominicans require "a heavy hand" to keep them under control is reflective of how Dominicans view themselves as "an unruly people" who continue to require a strong leader. Attitudes to violence, shaped by history, live on in the barrios as much as anywhere else. However, they are not necessarily identical to the attitudes held by outsiders: they are nuanced according to the circumstances of the people who profess them.

A VIEW FROM UNDER THE BRIDGE

Cienigüeros treat crime seriously and take measures to protect themselves. At eleven o'clock in the evening, people suddenly shut and bar their front doors. Given that doors are wide open during the day, this crossing of the threshold from freedom to lockdown is stark. After this hour, the only establishments open are colmadónes, grocery stores selling alcohol that blare music into the night while their patrons party on the concrete, open-air dance floors. Residents complain that they cannot leave anything outside the house because it will be missing the following morning. So great were Adela's fears of robbery in 2005 that she would enact an elaborate ritual of locking up her house. Lacking the "economic bonanza" that permits the middle classes to install elaborate

security systems and paid guards, Adela used everyday objects to secure
her home. First, she would bolt her front door and place a chair back
under the handle. Then, she would make her own audio alarm system
by balancing a crowbar upon the chair and placing glass bottles behind
the metal blinds on her windows. The idea was that if someone tried to
break in, these objects would fall onto the floor and wake her up (and
probably also her neighbors). Since the Barrio Seguro program, Adela
has pared down this ritual, no longer bothering with the crowbar and
bottles.

Residents talk daily about the problems of the barrio, sharing stories
of crimes and near misses, arrests and encounters, complaining about
the difficulties of living in La Ciénaga, and appraising new government
initiatives to improve services or combat crime. According to my 2005
survey of La Ciénaga, 66 percent of residents read the newspaper, 63
percent of households own a radio, and 73 percent own a television.
Residents are well aware of how the media and public view their community, and most agree that La Ciénaga is neither a desirable nor a safe
place to live. They learn about their dangerous status explicitly through
the nightly news, and they experience it implicitly through the "violence
of everyday life" (Scheper-Hughes 1992) as they encounter themselves
mirrored hierarchically in the body language and actions of others. In
many ways, the "talk of crime" within Santo Domingo's barrios directly
mirrors the perceptions presented in the media and by the public. Angelo told me:

> La Ciénaga is a barrio you can begin in. For people who have the
> wish to have something in their life it is a barrio where you can
> acquire a house with very little money, and from then on try to keep
> developing. There are very few positive things because it is a barrio
> where there is an abundance of delinquency, lots of drugs, lots of
> bars where they drink a lot and do innumerable other things. In
> reality it's a little bothersome, but one has to live in some place or
> other until one is able to advance.

When I asked cienigüeros what they considered to be the most negative aspects of their barrio, 68 percent identified delinquency, followed by pollution at 28 percent, robberies and thieves at 17 percent,
and drugs at 11 percent. In the context of La Ciénaga, *delinquency*
refers primarily to theft, fighting, shooting guns into the air, taking

drugs, and drinking excessively. The main difference between the responses of residents and outsiders to my surveys was that cienigüeros noted pollution as a major problem, whereas outsiders did not. They are referring to the rubbish that litters the streets and the open drains of black water that run through many areas of the community. Cienigüeros also referred less to police patrols than did either the general public or the media. Conversely, the most common responses to the open-ended question "What are the positive things about La Ciénaga?" were "nothing" (28 percent), "the barrio is being improved" (21 percent), "the schools" (17 percent), and "the churches" (13 percent). Many parents were hopeful that education would help their children find decent employment and move out of the barrios, but adults tended to be less hopeful for themselves, some telling me that they would remain in La Ciénaga until they died or the government relocated them.

However, residents do not condemn their barrio entirely. Although cienigüeros acknowledge the presence of danger, they oppose the way in which the talk of crime fails to recognize the respectability of the majority of residents. They argue, "We are not all delinquents; there are plenty of serious people in La Ciénaga." The public's and the media's view, in which the barrios are conflated as equally threatening, comes from their unwillingness to differentiate between types of danger. By identifying sources of danger, residents position it away from themselves and their community networks, claiming legitimacy as a community. The source of danger, thus identified, becomes easier to imagine, articulate, and manage.

Cienigüeros have methods to disassociate themselves from crime through various means, including externalizing its source. Residents of the different poor barrios tend to be suspicious of one another, and rarely consider their own barrio to be the most dangerous in the city. For example, residents of Guachupita asked me if it wasn't very dangerous for me to live in La Ciénaga, whereas cienigüeros took extra precautions against thieves when they visited Guachupita. According to various residents, La Ciénaga's internal problems are not caused by local young men, but rather by delinquents who visit the barrio from other, more dangerous barrios such as Guachupita, with the aim of committing crimes. In a modified version of this story, local delinquents have an arrangement with outsider delinquents whereby they commit crime in each other's barrios rather than their own, tipping each other off as to the best places to rob.

Other residents believe that danger exists within the barrio, but claim that their own sector is safe while others are dangerous. For example, one particular sector was widely agreed to be the most dangerous part of La Ciénaga. When I visited that sector, residents frequently told me that their own block was safe, but that a particular street within their sector was dangerous. When I visited that supposedly dangerous street and quizzed its residents, they told me that the street was perfectly safe except for one particular house where the delinquent lived. In this manner, residents continually maneuvered themselves out of negative representations by displacing the danger onto other spaces that they felt were at a social and physical distance. Streets or areas that hosted community buildings, such as schools and churches, were exempt from regional competition and were seen as positive and safe by all. Morally suspect or dangerous-looking spaces such as bars or abandoned buildings were believed to be unequivocally dangerous.

Danger is not always fixed in certain places, but rather moves around in relation to the self and others. As I walked around the barrio with one young man called Alex, he pointed down a street near the cliff and said, "Where we are now isn't dangerous, but see down this street? It's really dangerous down there." When I asked him why it was so dangerous, he answered, "Because down there they don't know me." In other words, familiarity breeds safety. Danger is not a constant property of other, immoral human beings. Rather, it is relative to the social self as one moves around a given spatial field. Social danger is also gendered and age-related: as a young man, he risked his safety by entering a new neighborhood that is dominated by groups of other young men. If he were a woman or an older man, he may not face the same threat. Men, rather than women, are more often perceived to be the perpetrators of violence. They are also victimized differently. While women can experience robberies and domestic abuse, men are far more commonly victims of homicide by civilians or police. However, it is difficult to make generalizations because whether one is subject to danger is very much dependent on the individual and their changing status over time. Felix told me in 2005 that because he was the first child born in the barrio and knows it very well, he can go anywhere without fear of danger. As of 2012 his privilege seemed to have changed, as a recent turnover in residents meant that many people no longer recognized him and, because he is light-skinned and well-dressed, would assume that he was an outsider. This misrecognition irritated him—as much as he would like to leave the barrio, he is proud of his place in its history. Symbolically cast out of the world he was born into, Felix feels that he is perched between two classes, and therefore not a full member of either.

CORRUPTION AND SOCIAL CLASS

Cienigüeros do not solely blame each other or state violence for the barrio's problems. The talk of crime also includes elements of social and political critique that addresses structural issues. According to my surveys and interviews, residents recognize the nation's precarious financial situation, while criticizing wasteful practices such as corruption, clientelism, the concentration of wealth among a small population, foreign ownership, low taxes, and extensive incentives to investors. The corruption of the wealthy and powerful is considered to have a direct effect on the moral well-being of the barrio, since it affects the ability of families to raise their children in a safe and secure environment:

> There are many lost young people and this hurts me because here there are many powerful people who could do something. There are children in the streets living below the bridge, in the parks, on the benches, and here in the country there are many people who could make schools and collect these children and take them to school. The politicians are only interested in politics and making money for themselves; they don't see what is happening in the streets, what is affecting us in the streets.
>
> If you have a headache and you don't look for medicine you're not going to get better. So if you come here and tell me, "Oh, my head hurts," then I'm going to say, "Well go look for a pill!" So if I take a pill my headache goes. I had the intention to get rid of my headache. The politicians come here campaigning for us to vote for them. After they get into power, if each one built a little piece of street we would live in gold, because here in this country there is money. This is a millionaire country, but there are no good intentions. Here there are millions and millions in the banks but for the street nothing, you see the politicians going around in jeeps but they don't help the barrios. (Angelo)

In other words, the Dominican Republic is a wealthy country, but the corruption of individuals prevents it from advancing. In many ways, the urban dreams of the poor correspond with normative imaginings of a comfortable life. If the archetypal rural character is a landed peasant who dances to merengue and has a large family, then the archetypal city person is an engineer or lawyer who listens to reggaetón, drives a Mercedes Benz, lives in a planned neighborhood, and takes trips to Miami and New York. Barrio residents' aspirations for the future include dreams of material wealth: the modernization of the barrio, salaries that allow consumption of consumer goods, and transnational lifestyles characterized by movement between diffuse places.

However, residents' dreams are not limited to reproducing traditional class relations and superimposing themselves as beneficiaries. While barrio residents covet good-quality housing situated in well-serviced, safe neighborhoods, they view the wealthy as prone to illness because of their antisocial lifestyle. When I undertook my survey of the barrio, I was struck by the number of residents who told me, "Us poor people have more freedom than the rich, because we can go wherever we like without worrying about getting robbed." Indeed, the constraints on the rich were seen not just as security measures but also pathological. As numerous cienigüeros told me, "The rich have to walk around with security guards and are always getting sick through constantly worrying about their money."

This critique of the wealthy does not just concern practical issues of safety truncating freedoms, but also infers that the poor are innately more moral than the wealthy. Cienigüeros quoted to me on more than one occasion the Christian Bible's warning that "it is easier for a camel to pass through the eye of a needle than for a rich man to enter the kingdom of heaven" (Luke 18:25). They may not drive a BMW, but they believe that they are in closer communication with God. However, the poor are not immune to dreams of wealth and heightened consumption, and according to some residents, these aspirations can have negative social effects. Geovanny, a community leader, protests that while politicians steal and break promises, parents are equally culpable because they work long hours to be able to meet an ever-increasing minimum standard of living and neglect their children:

The rich can pay for their children to go to a nursery, but us poor have to leave them alone in the house to look after themselves as well as they can. While we are in the street working, they are doing whatever they feel like because there are no adults watching them. This is why our society is so corrupt, with so much delinquency, so much crime and ugly things, the lack of care on the part of the parents.

I always say that us parents are responsible for delinquency, because if your children aren't watched they will follow the wrong path. I don't blame them but rather us. Us and globalization, as before we didn't have televisions because we couldn't buy them, but now every poor person has a twenty-inch television in their house, a huge stereo, a VHS, and a fridge, everything. Parents have left their children behind to go and achieve what they want, what they wish, to scale the ladder. Before it was Father and Mother before everything. Material goods have diverted us from parenting.

By segueing from the local to the global and back again, Geovanny demonstrates how residents turn their awareness of structural inequalities back onto the individual. As I will describe in the following chapter, barrio residents tend to reproduce the class ideologies that bind them in place and stigmatize them, despite being aware of the injustices of poverty and marginalization. Just as La Ciénaga is stigmatized as "abajo el puente" by other city residents, cienigüeros divide their own barrio and its residents into a moral geography of high and low spaces characterized by features of landscape, racial appearance, and consumption practices. In this dualism, certain spaces and their residents are deemed less moral than others. However, it competes with an alternative value system in which dualistic categories of place and personhood are conflated into normative categories. In the following chapter I detail how cienigüeros negotiate these conflicting values through material practices and symbolism.

6

FLEXIBLE IDENTITIES

Negotiating Values through Material Forms

Back in 2005, when she was working as a domestic servant, Morena would spend her evenings in the living room of Adela's house. The two women, one thirty-something and dark skinned, the other in her seventies and indio, would sit on plastic chairs and gossip by candlelight, enjoying the sea breeze flowing freely through the open louvers and doors. Their conversation was frequently punctuated by the occasional needs of Morena's three young children, visiting friends and relatives, or perhaps a neighbor looking to buy one of Adela's bottles of home-made juice. Visitors would stop by for a few minutes to share news: whether the men were finding much work in construction, whether the new police station was dissuading the delincuentes, or whether the barrio was just as **caliente** *(hot, troublesome) as ever.*

On one occasion, Adela and Morena, along with Ariano and Diego (Adela's nephews), were discussing a robbery at the billiard club near the barrio's entrance. The robbery was on a Sunday night, the busiest night of the week, when the club is packed with locals dancing to bacha-ta and reggaetón. According to Ariano, a gang of thirty young men from a neighboring barrio held up the club at gunpoint at around one o'clock in the morning. They made everyone put their hands up, confiscated all the men's guns, robbed wallets and the till, and then liberated motor-bikes outside by shooting the chains so they could drive off on them.

"But the military station is just across the road from the club," said Morena, "Didn't they do anything?" (The military station is a leftover from when the barrio was blockaded under Balaguer between 1991 and 1996.)

"Of course they didn't!" responded ever-cynical Adela in disgust. "Don't be stupid, Morena. They have a deal with the delincuentes. Neither the military nor the police are ever going to do anything around here."

Ariano turned to me with a twinkle in his eye. "It's a hot barrio, isn't it Erin?" he asked. "Not like how you told me about Tokyo, where there are no thieves." Ariano had been highly amused when I told him that in Tokyo people leave their bicycles unchained on the street while they work all day in high-rise offices, and he repeated the story to anyone who would listen.

Adela ignored him. "The barrio is getting worse and worse," she stated emphatically. "Before you could walk around anywhere, but now we have to restrict our movements in our own barrio. Abajo is filled with tígueres, Haitians, and thieves. I hardly leave the house except to go to the market or the church. When Eduardo visits he comes the long way on his scooter so as not to pass through abajo." Eduardo, Adela's son, has since been resettled, but he used to live in Guachupita, a barrio that is one of the most frequently reported trouble spots in the media. Much to my surprise, Eduardo once described Guachupita to me as "very hot right now, but not as hot as La Ciénaga."

While Adela was talking, Carmencita, a slight, forty-year-old Haitian woman, entered the yard on her way home from a meeting at CODECI. Carmencita didn't take Adela's objection to Haitians seriously, having been a neighbor and a friend of Adela's for nearly thirty years.

"Adela, you shouldn't let the thieves stop you. This is our barrio! Look at me, I'm small and I go everywhere and at all hours!"

"She's right," interjected Morena. "I usually come home from work in the dark and nothing has ever happened to me. I think that if you have confidence and believe that nothing will happen to you, then nothing will."

"You're kidding yourself," Adela responded. "In no part of this barrio is there tranquility. Here arriba in La Clarín is the only part that is relatively tranquil right now."

"*That's not true, Adela,*" *retorted Carmencita.* "*I walk around the barrio every day and in all parts there are many who are working for the community—good people, serious people. The thieves and delinquents are only a minority.*"

Ariano looked mischievous. "*Yes, there are many people who should be taken seriously—they are armed!*"

If this dialogue appears to closely resemble the way that outsiders talk about La Ciénaga, it is because it does. Barrio residents reproduce among themselves the stigma that is placed on the barrio as a whole. Just as outsiders differentiate between the low land occupied by the barrios and the high land occupied by the rest of the city, cienigüeros divide up their own community into high and low spaces. Whereas residents of the high land claim respectability, the low land has a bad reputation and is stigmatized through association with poverty, darker skin, wasteful consumption, and immorality. Residents of the high land especially mobilize this divide to distance themselves from the problems that are projected onto their barrio, casting themselves as "serious people" in contrast to the "delincuentes" who occupy the low land and give the barrio its bad reputation. These value judgments draw on national values, but in Santo Domingo and La Ciénaga they have particular geographic and material manifestations. Forms of dress, kinds of housing, distinctive spaces, and people's bodies act as canvases on which identities are constructed, and by which people are judged. That is to say, cienigüeros draw on all three domains of materiality (bodies, objects, and spaces) to reproduce the very categories that are used against the barrio by outsiders.

Yet this is not the end of the story. What is most interesting about this practice of dualism is that it sits alongside an alternative value system, adhered to nationwide, that provides the means for people to overturn their exclusion and claim group membership. This alternative value system contends that Dominican culture is founded not on difference, but on three normative categories of personhood. The first is the racial category of indio, which classifies the vast majority of Dominicans as belonging to *la raza dominicana* (the Dominican race). The second is a social class category, ***clase media*** (middle class), to which a surprising number of cienigüeros claim to belong. The third is the persona of the tíguere, a kind of trickster who is simultaneously a national hero and a morally dubious person. These categories are central to Dominican culture and reflect the nation's high level of creolization—the blending of identity categories over the centuries.

Cienigüeros (and, in fact, most Dominicans) practice these two opposing value systems simultaneously, which makes for a lively field of identity politics. On the one hand, dualism generates a very clear power dynamic in which individuals claim a monopoly on morality and respectability by representing other people as immoral. On the other hand, normative categories of personhood are startlingly flexible in terms of who they can admit. For example, it only requires a small cognitive shift for a delincuente to be recategorized as a tíguere, or a moreno as an indio. Furthermore, some residents challenge spatial dualism directly, by refusing to reproduce the division of space according to morality. Both dualism and normativity offer ways to play with values, the social positions they confer, and the spaces in which they operate. In this chapter I examine how these value systems are practiced through the manipulation of materiality and its symbolism.

CREOLIZING DUALISMS

Dualisms of various kinds have been identified in different Caribbean countries, and were originally thought to have emerged from the socially devastating effects of the transatlantic slave trade and the vast inequalities instituted between Africans and Europeans. To justify slavery, Europeans developed a dualism that posited white and black as moral opposites. This legacy lived on in various forms around the region. Possibly the most well-known cultural dualism in the Caribbean is described in Peter Wilson's (1973) ethnography *Crab Antics*. According to Wilson, life on the island of Providencia, off the coast of Colombia, entails two parallel value complexes that residents draw on to create their social identities. One is "respectability," characterized by European-derived indicators of status such as education, monogamy, church attendance, and family life. Respectability is mostly sought after by the upper classes, light-skinned people, and women. The second is "reputation," characterized by flexibility and ingenuity in order to survive, promiscuity, and street life. It is practiced more by the lower classes, darker-skinned people, and men. Reputation is not necessarily immoral;

rather, it is an alternative way of constructing identity and gaining social status. Wilson argues that the Creole population invented the practice of reputation as an alternative to European values.

Daniel Miller (1994) has a different hypothesis about how cultural dualism began. On the basis of his ethnographic research in Trinidad, he suggests that the source of Wilson's dualism may not be the differentiation of colonial and Creole values. Rather, its source may lie in modernity itself and its articulations with Caribbean history. Modernity is characterized by a temporal consciousness of movement and change, but also by a search for "rootedness" or stability, which people find in their cultural traditions. Globally, this split does not inevitably result in dualism, but it has appeared in the Caribbean due to the region's intensive experiences of change and rupture, especially resulting from production in slavery and indentured labor. Trinidad has developed a unique national identity that is based on ethnic dualism and is a response to the conditions of modernity as experienced in the region, rather than a response to colonial powers. One of dualism's precursors that is specific to Trinidad is a sense of rapid change created by Trinidad's oil boom (circa 1976–1983). Its demise instilled feelings of insecurity, which heightened a search for rootedness, or transcendence, amid modernity's transience. Consumption provides a way to reconcile dualism, as objects can simultaneously express both tradition and change.

However, creolization is also a feature of Caribbean life. In the Dominican Republic, dualisms sit alongside creolized categories developed through nationalistic movements, especially encouraged by the state. The coexistence of dualisms and creolizations means that people are not perpetually confined to one of two opposing categories: one does not have to be black or white, rich or poor, respectable or a delinquent. Instead, all of these oppositions are tempered by the existence of a third category that erases difference and creates the basis for social unity.

Race is a case in point. Settled by fairly equal numbers of Europeans and Africans, the Dominican population has mixed to a large degree. The terms *black* and *white* underwrite notions of morality, yet virtually everyone can claim to fit into the Creole category of "indio," or be placed there by others at a whim. The few who are considered to not be indio are also often considered to not be Dominican: "Haitians" are considered to be black, and "Americans" are assumed to be white. The sociologist Karin Weyland, in a series of videos she made while at the Fundación Melassa in Santo Domingo, visually demonstrates how racial self-identification operates when she asks people on the streets of Santo Domingo what color they are. Virtually all respondents answered "indio," despite the fact that they cover a broad spectrum of colors. Where racial self-identification is concerned, there is no dualism: the majority of people describe themselves in normative terms. Yet, in daily speech, Dominicans use a plurality of racial terms to both insult each other and show affection. For example, while it is common to assume that criminals are "morenos," many families nickname their darkest-skinned child "moreno" or "morena." It is, as Aisha Khan (2004) describes for Trinidad, a rainbow with teeth: simultaneously beautiful and dangerous.

Class and character also have normative categories. During my survey of La Ciénaga, I was astonished to find how many people identified as "middle class" with explanations such as "because I eat every day," "because I have a refrigerator," or "because there are many people who are worse off than I am." Again, while people self-identify in this fashion, it is unusual for cienigüeros to classify each other as middle class. In my experience, they are more likely to describe each other as "poor" or "mas o menos" (more or less okay). It is even less likely that outsiders would agree with this "middle-class" classification, given that they view barrio residents as summarily poor.

Dualisms and normative categories of personhood have material effects, especially when it comes to their spatialization within the barrio. Specifically, their performance is shaped by particular geographic features of Santo Domingo and La Ciénaga. While dualism in the Dominican Republic incorporates a range of cultural values, they are overlaid on these city spaces in a way that makes it difficult to untangle them from their material manifestations.

ARRIBA AND ABAJO: THE SPATIALIZATION OF DIFFERENCE

La Ciénaga's spatial dualism does not just classify and value spaces: it imposes moral judgments onto people. Whereas the nationwide "talk of crime" blames the barrios for the nation's social ills, the talk of crime within La Ciénaga commonly identifies abajo as being the primary source of moral corruption. This kind of shifting of blame to particular spaces is not at all uncommon in urban centers. In fact, Harvey proposes that these "moral geographies" are universal. He remarks,

> No social group can subsist without a working knowledge of the definition and qualities of its territory, of its environment, of its "situated identity" in the world. . . . Every individual and every social group possesses, therefore, a distinctive "geographical lore" and "geographical praxis," some loosely structured body of knowledge and experience about matters geographical. The social transmission of that knowledge is vital to the perpetuation or transformation of any social order. (Harvey 2000, 551–52)

Harvey asserts, citing state department politics in the United States, that these moral geographies commonly operate by "demon[izing] spaces and places" (2000, 552). In times of rapid change and instability, this process of differentiation and identification becomes more intense. A series of economic crises from the early 1980s resulted in polarization of the poor and wealthy, which is expressed idiomatically in terms of arriba and abajo. Similarly, a national ideology separating dominicanidad from haitianismo emerged out of the violent separation of the Dominican Republic from Haiti in 1844. While this emergence of dualism from crisis was noted by Miller for Trinidad and Wilson for Providencia, Santo Domingo's dualism diverges in that it rests on a distinctive moral geography. La Ciénaga's natural geography differs markedly between its high and low parts, lending itself naturally to qualitative judgments. Given the barrio's tendency to flood, the higher parts have historically been the most suitable sites in which to construct houses. Even today, when storm drains carry vast quantities of tropical rain out of the barrio and into the river, there are still parts of the barrio that flood, and places where concrete houses literally sink into the swamp as the soggy ground cannot support their weight.

Arriba consists of the high land in the center of the barrio, the main street leading to the barrio's entrance, and the cliffs separating La Ciénaga from Guachupita. The vast majority of houses located arriba are built of concrete block, the area does not flood, and most of the barrio's services are located in these areas. La Clarín, the hill in the middle of the barrio, is the most desirable area to live in because it houses the school, the Catholic Church, and the CODECI's office. It also has the highest rate of church attendance out of the barrio's six sectors.

Abajo consists of the swampy central ground in between the hill and the cliff, and the land around the edge of the river. Besides flooding, abajo exhibits a greater degree of poverty in its built environment. It tends to be far more crowded with houses, accessed by narrow alley-ways, and more difficult to access than the higher land. With few roads wide enough for vehicles, entire rows of houses have been known to burn to the ground as fire trucks cannot get in to put out the blaze. Building materials that are common abajo exacerbate the danger of fires: there are still many wood and tin houses, and fabric is often used to line internal walls. The risk of fire is compounded by the irregular electricity supply as residents often depend on candles and oil lamps in the evenings.

In terms of social life, abajo is infamous for its **colmadónes** (open-air bars), whose noise and revelry place them firmly in the domain of reputation. The rowdiest colmadónes are located off the main streets and they draw their clientele from neighbors who live close by. Colmadónes occupy a similar place in Dominican life as dancehalls in Jamaica. They are places for the (relatively) young and (somewhat) disreputable, particularly men, to gather, drink beer and rum, listen to reggaetón and bachata, and flirt. Every weekend, the sounds of partying float up to La Clarín from abajo, occasionally accompanied by gunshots. Often their activity will be audible the following morning. "Listen to the tígueres!" Felix regularly exclaimed. "Listen to the state of disorder that this country is in!" For Felix and his brother Marco, the partying abajo is indicative of a disintegration of the Dominican people, who have fallen into *corrupción* (corruption, meaning immorality) in hard times, rather than persevering with traditional peasant values of hard work and austerity.

Race is also an intrinsic part of the barrio's moral geography, as a commonly held assumption is that the majority of residents of abajo are dark-skinned Dominicans and Haitians. This perception of racial differ-ence has a tenuous basis in reality. Arriba was occupied in the 1970s by somewhat lighter-skinned migrants from Cibao, whereas abajo was pri-marily occupied in the 1980s by somewhat darker-skinned migrants from Pedernales. However, given the flexibility of the Dominican racial classification system, it is possible that place of residence prompts racial labeling, rather than the other way around. In other words, one could argue that dark-skinned people are labeled as "moreno" because they live abajo; if they lived arriba, they may well be labeled "indio." Nor is nationality as clear a marker of difference as it seems. In 2012 I undertook a small study of self-identified Haitians living in La Ciénaga. The results indicated that there is a tendency for the children of Haitian migrants to identify themselves as Haitian, even if they are Dominican-born, have Dominican citizenship, and have never been to Haiti. This is partly because of the insistence of Dominicans in singling out Haitians, but also because Haitians are often proud of their origins and, according to my young interviewees, are reviving Haitian cultural activities in the Dominican Republic's urban centers. Given that La Ciénaga's moral geography is a complex mix of values and identities, residents are constantly pushed to renegotiate their position within it, regardless of their claim on respectability.

RESPECTABILITY ON HIGH

Whether described in terms of respectability and reputation (Wilson 1973), inside and outside lives (Austin 1984), or transience and transcendence (Miller 1994), dualism suggests that throughout Caribbean societies there are two opposed methods by which individuals can seek out social status, recognition, and power. Who chooses which method may depend on social class, ethnicity, gender, and age. However, while dualism holds some explanatory power over how binary categories operate, people do not always engage with dualism in a dualistic fashion. Wilson's rendering of dualism acknowledges that people use both respectability and reputation simultaneously, but it does not explain why.

Adela's life story is a useful of example of how—and why—people may draw on both reputation and respectability at key moments in their lives and fortunes. Today, Adela's engagement with respectability and reputation is most visible in her attitudes to the barrio's moral geography. One fine afternoon, I stood with Adela outside the front of her house as she surveyed the street. The night before, I had been interviewing her about her life history, and she was in a reflective mood. Commenting on how much the barrio has changed since she first arrived in 1972, she remarked that she no longer has to wear Wellington boots to pass through abajo on her way to the market. Nevertheless, she continues to avoid the lowlands, which she views as rambling, unhealthy, and dangerous. Adela prefers to stay close to home in La Clarín, where she has built a decent concrete home near her family and the Catholic church. Having built her stable position despite her poverty and minimal schooling, Adela has always been self-sufficient, and is understandably cynical regarding the ability of the state or other political organizations to provide assistance and a route to progress. In daily practice, Adela's social radius is centered on the street on which she lives, limiting her visits abajo to activities relating to her livelihood or her involvement with the Catholic Church. She is reluctant to place her trust in anyone but her family and the church. Indeed, Adela and Maria often claim that the church *is* their family: the church has been the most prominent institutional presence in their lives, and many members of the congregation have lived in La Ciénaga for decades. Adela goes to Mass two or three times per week, attends prayer meetings weekly, and partakes in special events such as Easter processions.

Adela's history tells a different story of engagement with reputation, one that goes far beyond the moral geography of La Ciénaga and Santo Domingo. Despite her aspirations to respectability, Adela has a history of engagement with reputation that continues to form her practice, if not her discourse, to the same degree. After years of attending church activities abajo, Adela knows a great deal more of the barrio than she commonly lets on. Moreover, Adela's conservatism hides a life history characterized by activities that can be described as belonging to the domain of reputation—a series of courageous and creative searches for solutions to her problems that involved going against social norms that limit women to the domestic sphere and insist that they are dependent upon men. Adela, throughout her life, has exhibited as least as much **tigüeraje** as she has normative respectability, though according to Adela, she was driven more by necessity and a search for autonomy than an aspiration to leave the domestic sphere. As a poor teenager in Cibao, Adela was engaged to a moreno man who she did not particularly like. This was in the 1940s, during the second decade of the Trujillo era, when it was illegal to travel without a national identity card. Adela was unable to leave her home in the countryside because she was not yet old enough to apply for a card. When she turned sixteen (in 1948), she immediately obtained one, told her fiance that she was going on a short trip to the city to visit relatives, and caught a bus to the capital with her wedding trousseau in hand. Once there, Adela sold the sheets, clothes, and household goods that her fiance had given to her and used the money to establish herself in the city.

Over the next two decades, Adela worked as a domestic servant, married twice, and had four children. By the time she moved from Guachupita to La Ciénaga with her children in 1972, Adela was again single. Relocating to La Ciénaga was an opportunity to make a home with other family members close by. In the 1980s, she reluctantly migrated to Venezuela to work as a domestic servant, motivated only by the thought of improving her family's economic situation. For Adela, the move was risky: to uproot oneself from one's family, community, and country required courage and determination. But, despite the hardships she experienced in her fifteen years in Caracas, Adela managed to fulfill her goal of making enough money to build a house in La Ciénaga (as I described in chapter 2). Adela used reputation—taking advantage of risk and mobility—to gain the economic resources necessary to attain respectability. Today, Adela's primary aim is to enjoy the security and social position she has gained. Having had to engage so much with reputation's insecurities throughout her career, she is now reluctant to travel far from home and never visits her remaining relatives in the country. Her only trips out of Santo Domingo are church excursions, including a yearly picnic by a river.

Adela's neighbor Morena, in her thirties, is engaging with the tussle between respectability and reputation that Adela, now well into her seventies, found necessary to establish herself. Morena's behavior is very much aligned with values of reputation, including being street-savvy, willing to transgress moral-spatial boundaries, and entrepreneurial. Like Adela, her performance of tigüeraje is a strategy to maintain a modicum of respectability. Morena's primary concern is that the reputation she and most other adults engage in may corrupt her children. She worries that her young daughters will become **mujeres sin vergüenza** (shameless women), and her son a thief, because they spend much of their time playing with other children on the street without parental supervision. A few years ago, she secured a job working for *Ciudad Limpia* (Clean City), a government program that hires barrio residents to pick up rubbish on the city's streets. Dressed in bright-orange work overalls, Morena works from seven in the morning until two in the afternoon. She is relieved to have given up her long hours working as a domestic servant so that she can be home in the afternoons to look after her children. Her youngest son, Jeury, was a serious and studious child when I first met him at eight years of age. Now sixteen, he continues to excel at school and is constantly seeking to learn from his peers, especially young men who are slightly older than him. Recently, he and a few local friends of about the same age decided to launch fledgling careers as hip-hop artists. They began putting on performances in the local park and recorded their own CDs. These teenagers style themselves along the line of gangster culture, pulling tough poses for photographs. Their parents, far from being interpreted as idolizing crime, encourage their creativity and hope that it can one day bear economic fruit. Tigüeraje and its movimiento provides many possible paths to progreso, including incorporating the global equivalent of the Dominican Republic's tigüeraje.

Adela's and Morena's stories suggest that an individual's engagement with respectability and reputation is fundamentally an economic one: if either woman had sufficient resources, they would not have to engage in practices of reputation at all. Yet I feel that this interpretation does not do justice to their own experiences and values, let alone the next generation's. Adela and Morena are clearly not univalent beings who wish to live the gendered "inside" life of a middle-class family, which many view as isolating. Rather, they are vivacious, independent women whose brand of respectability is not merely a desire to emulate the middle class. Like the more privileged classes, they would like to be able to choose how they engage with respectability and reputation, particularly as socioeconomic changes increase the uncertainties of everyday life.

In the context of poverty and the stigmatization of the barrios, respectability could also be seen as oppositional in the sense that they struggle against the life of reputation that they have been born into, and according to which media and public opinion continue to represent them. What is clear is that despite the fact that cienigüeros pitch the respectability of arriba against the reputation of abajo, it is rare, if not unknown, to find a person who does not engage in both simultaneously. In other words, there is a quantum leap between discourse and practice. How people choose to engage with respectability and reputation depends in large part on their individual circumstances, more than their gender, racial identity, nationality, or age.

MAN OF THE HOUSE

Adela's concern for respectability and domesticity is by no means exclusive to women. In the urban milieu, being an **hombre de la casa** (man of the house) takes on a particular salience as a means of distancing oneself from social degradation associated with poor barrios. While Dominican notions of masculinity are centered on reputation and the street, men also aspire to respectability and use reputation strategically to achieve it. In some ways, getting this juggling act right can be pressing for men because they struggle with negative notions of masculinity—especially criminalization—as they attempt to balance the risks and benefits of reputation with their aspirations for respectability.

Adela's cousin Cristino, who is in his late eighties, is a good example of respectability's lengthy presence among working class men. Cristino has never sought to be a man of reputation despite having lived in the city (the main site of tigüeraje) since his early twenties. Cristino has been devoutly religious since he was a young man, and his family and the Catholic Church are central to his respectability. In my interviews with him detailing his life history, his dialogue is punctuated at intervals with prayers. Until he went blind in 2008, Cristino attended Mass twice weekly and read his bible every day. Cristino views himself as coming from a poor but respectable family:

> The men in my family live simply, thanks to God. I don't drink. I don't dance. I don't hang around in the street. I am a man of the house, not a shameless man, a charlatan. We aren't the type of men who chase women. Perhaps one is poor, but to be poor isn't a sin.

Cristino's description of his family's men presents them as distinctly *not* in the realm of reputation; nor does he give any apologies for not conforming to what Wilson viewed as a central component of male working-class Caribbean life. He associates domesticity with religion, claiming that poverty is no excuse for living a licentious life. One may not have resources, but one can find solace in family and God, rather than partaking in the street's corrupción. Yet, like Adela, Cristino has lived a mobile and colorful life. He migrated to the city when he was a young man and spent many years working at odd jobs. He is a gifted orator and tells a repertoire of stories involving run-ins with authority, and movement between the city and the country. Cristino was arrested twice for not carrying an identity card, once under Trujillo and again under Balaguer. Each time he spent three days or so in La Victoria, Santo Domingo's notorious jail that is featured in the book and film *La Fiesta del Chivo* (*The Feast of the Goat*) (2000) by Mario Vargas Llosa. He tells how on another occasion, when he was thirty-five years of age, he escaped arrest:

> There was a group of Trujillo's assassins called The Owls who would do damage by night. If they found people on the street from ten o'clock in the evening onwards they would blow them away. And this one day, normally I would be home by then but I was out late. I had to walk eight kilometers home because [public] cars were hard to come by at that hour.
>
> So, I was walking down the street when they came upon me. I was scared but I told them, "I haven't done anything wrong or suspicious." They were tall and one was prieto [black]. Another had blue eyes. He looked at me and said, "He seems like a man who is searching for work." I had a hammock to sleep in and a machete. They didn't ask me anything; they just turned around and left! So I went running in the other direction so that when they returned they wouldn't find me there. I ran to my house, which was already close by, and I stayed there.

Cristino's story demonstrates a conflict between the dictatorship's agenda and the realities of everyday life. Trujillo was the great domesticator: in his bid to control Dominican life entirely, he restricted freedom of movement and, through state violence, made the streets dangerous for ordinary people (Derby 1998). But in controlling movement, he limited men's ability to earn a livelihood and increased their need to be courageous and take risks, a central feature of Dominican masculinity. Throughout his life, Cristino has had to take many risks, but like Adela, most were more from necessity than choice, and he settled on a domestic life as soon as he was able. Cristino's religiosity throughout his life has been a way of coping with the stresses and uncertainties of poverty.

It does not diminish his masculinity; rather, it instills respect in him as a serious man.

Cristino's sons, Felix and Marco, have also adopted a home-centered stance, socializing primarily with their family and nearby friends. On most afternoons they gather with some of their male relatives in the backyard to share news and drink strong, sweet Dominican coffee. Marco and Felix may visit other people in the evenings, but more commonly they stay at home to receive a regular swathe of visitors. Their parents' house is something of a locus for family and friends to hablar vaina and organize cooperative work on their houses. Both Marco and Felix follow their father's example and restrict their movements to the barrio's main streets, unless they have a good reason to visit abajo. Their mother, Maria, discourages them from walking around abajo at night for fear that they will be arrested, or even murdered, by trigger-happy police. Local events such as the robbery of the pool hall can also be a disincentive to movement and street life. Marco refuses to visit the billiards club at the entrance to the barrio, claiming that it is too caliente. Felix is not as cautious as Marco: he argues that he knows all the delincuentes, so they will not rob or shoot him unless they do not recognize him because they are on drugs. His ability to navigate abajo or return from the city late at night requires local social knowledge, including familiarity with the local *motoconchistas* (motorbike taxi drivers).

Although Felix is protective of his respectability, he deploys a number of reputation's characteristics, including shrewdness, adaptability, flexibility, oral skills, and mobility. In essence, Felix enacts a form of masculinity that is normative for the middle class, shunning elements associated with working-class reputation. He aspires to gain good employment and a middle-class lifestyle, which would allow him to move to a better suburb and immerse himself in the social world on a voluntary rather than an obligatory basis. In contrast to Felix, Marco's aspirations center on staying in La Ciénaga. While he has many ideas for how to progress, he is conservative in their implementation. In some ways, Marco defends his respectability too closely. This is evident in conversation between his mother, Maria, and Adela at the beginning of chapter 2, when Maria and Adela expressed frustration at Marco's difficulties finding employment. In their view, Marco loses opportunities for advancement because he does not take risks. Being an hombre de la casa is a legitimate goal, but the women are well aware that the practice of reputation is often necessary to secure respectability. It is a fine line to tread, requiring the deployment of enough reputation to increase one's life chances, but not so much that one slips from tigüeraje into delincuencia. However, there are certainly people in La Ciénaga who manage to not just walk the line but to break it down altogether.

WALKING IN BETWEEN

Carmencita offers some intriguing differences to other practitioners of respectability. As a member of the Catholic Church and a Haitian, she is implicated on both sides of the barrio's dualism. Carmencita openly challenges the barrio's moral geography by maintaining her right to respectability despite her nationality and her insistence on moving freely through the barrio's spaces. She is not alone in this quest. Within La Ciénaga, the Catholic Church in particular works to combat discrimination against Haitians by preaching equality and running various groups for Haitian members of the congregation. In La Ciénaga, the church helps Dominican-born children obtain birth certificates, run a Haitian choir (currently directed by a Haitian priest), hold a monthly Mass in Haitian Creole in the church in Guachupita, and administer a Haitian refugee service in Centro Bonó. They also redraw the barrio's symbolic order, such as by holding Mass in the yards of members scattered throughout the barrio.

Carmencita and her older sister, Digna, are two of the Church's most committed members in La Ciénaga, spending much of their time **trabajando para la comunidad** (working for the community), a task that involves extensive knowledge of the barrio and networking with its people. Their church activities have formed an important part of the struggles they faced in the early years as Haitians living in the Dominican Republic, in terms of both gaining respect from their neighbors, and achieving tasks such as enrolling their children in school.

Carmencita was brought up by her godmother in Marigot, a pretty, beachside town in Haiti's south, where she attended Mass and helped her godmother run a small shop. Digna grew up with their parents on a small farm in the hills. Despite Carmencita's more advantageous position in town, she did not learn to read and write, while her elder sister is literate. When Carmencita was fourteen, her godmother died, and Carmencita returned to live with her parents. She continued attending Mass and was confirmed. Carmencita moved to La Ciénaga in 1981, when she was still a teenager. She married a Haitian man, and currently lives with two of her own children (who have Dominican citizenship), and two of her younger sister's children (who have not been naturalized). Digna moved from Haiti to La Ciénaga in 1984, and three of their other siblings followed soon thereafter. All settled in La Ciénaga.

As a poor, black, Haitian woman, Carmencita possesses many of the hallmarks of Dominican marginalization. Despite gaining respect, she remains to some extent an outsider. This is not entirely a negative position to occupy, as it grants her a degree of flexibility to contest social boundaries. In this respect she possesses the benefits and drawbacks of being what sociologist Georg Simmel calls a "stranger":

> He is fixed within a particular spatial group, or within a group whose boundaries are similar to spatial boundaries. But his position in this group is determined, essentially, by the fact that he has not belonged to it from the beginning, that he imports qualities into it, which do not and cannot stem from the group itself. (cited in Wolff 1950, 402)

Carmencita embodies the "distance and nearness, indifference and involvement" (Simmel, cited in Wolff 1950, 404) that Simmel identifies as the qualities of the stranger. While she has lived in La Ciénaga for three decades and is deeply involved in its community networks, Carmencita still remains a stranger in certain key respects. She adds qualities that are not local in that she has a different appearance due to her Haitian features and dress (though this is contextual), speaks Kreyol as well as Spanish, and expresses divergent opinions, including championing mobility for women and insisting on the value of Haitian culture. She is more mobile than most Dominicans, especially women. She regularly takes trips to visit relatives in different parts of the Dominican Republic and her parents back in Haiti. Indeed, female mobility is far more common in Haiti, where women run the domestic market system and import cheap goods from Panama and China. Carmencita and her sister are also unusually mobile within the barrio. As a result of their many activities, Carmencita and Digna are rarely found at home in the afternoons. Their commitment and mobility do not go unnoticed, and many community women remark of Carmencita and Digna that "these wom-

en don't stop at home!" These remarks express both an admiration for
the sisters' commitment to the Church and a concern for their well-
being. Conversely, Carmencita and Digna joke that Dominican women
are lazy and housebound compared to Haitian women.

Simmel wrote that the stranger cannot be an "owner of soil," and,
while Carmencita owns a house, her right to own it has been contested
by those around her. Originally, both sisters settled abajo, but around
five years ago Carmencita and her husband secured a plot of land on
the edge of La Clarín. It is a tiny, three-room, concrete house that they
built themselves with money her husband earned selling clothes in the
city market. Their neighbors were jealous that Haitians could own a
"good" house, while many Dominicans could not. One evening soon
after the house was built, a drunken neighbor threatened to kill them,
saying that they had no right to be living there. The next day, Carmencita took out a court order against her neighbor, and he was forced to face
a legal authority for adjudication of the dispute. He apologized to Carmencita and never bothered her again. Indeed, the house is a point of
pride for Carmencita. Technically it is located on low ground, but its
main access point is via the high ground, so Carmencita can legitimately
claim to reside arriba. She takes pride in her La Clarín residence and
the status it offers her, particularly since her "good" house and her
residential location allow her to defy common stereotypes of Haitians as
occupying the worst parts of the barrio and the worst houses.

Not all Haitians manage to resolve their problems with Dominicans
so easily, however. Recounting an incident on a sugar plantation where
a Haitian *bracero* (cane worker) had entrusted his savings to a Dominican who subsequently betrayed him and stole the money, Carmencita
defended her right to belong:

> If a Dominican sees that a Haitian has a good house, you know what
> they do? They look for trouble with them; they kill them or whatever,
> so that they can take it from them. If I struggle and manage to build
> my house then nobody should abuse me or ask for my [immigration]
> papers. Leonel's [President Fernandez] government should take ac-
> count of this.

Here Carmencita draws a clear link between the treatment of Haitians
at the national level and their ability to belong in local communities.
She suggests that if the Dominican government did not harass Haitians,

they would command the same respect as Dominicans for having struggled to obtain a good house. Carmencita feels that her family's position in the barrio is threatened because regular state deportations encourage Dominicans to treat Haitians badly, regardless of their legal status. For Digna and Carmencita, the ability of the Church to help their children to fight against the state was a major draw-card to joining the Church:

> When I didn't know the Catholic Church I worked hard trying to enroll my children in school. All my life has been work; I worked hard when I didn't know the Catholic Church. Now I have been attending for eleven years. How should I tell you? The church is like my home. I feel very good in it and they help me with anything. They helped me enroll my Haitian children in the school, as they didn't have birth certificates. (Carmencita)

Indeed, in the Dominican Republic, thousands of Haitian and Dominican children are excluded from school because they do not have birth certificates to prove their nationality. Under the Dominican constitution, children born in the Dominican Republic used to automatically be Dominican citizens, but it has not been uncommon for hospitals to refuse to issue birth certificates to children of Haitian parents, or for authorities to be uncooperative in producing such certificates. Over the years, Digna and Carmencita have worked with the church to obtain papers for dozens of Haitian and Dominican children. The rights of Haitian immigrants were restricted after the earthquake that devastated Port-au-Prince on January 12, 2010, compelled considerable numbers of refugees to relocate to the Dominican Republic.

Carmencita's illiteracy places few restrictions on her involvement in church organizations, because her sociability and competence make her well suited to community work on the ground. I accompanied Carmencita in many of her activities, including church-run classes on pregnancy health and childcare. Prenatal classes for pregnant women (the *Pastoral Materno-Infantil*) are held once per fortnight in the school. Every month, the counselors visit the homes of the women assigned to them to check on their well-being and update their cards. Carmencita uses these visits to conduct other business she has in the barrio, mapping out a route that also includes a selection of friends and relatives, people from the church's Haitian choir, parents of children who needed to obtain birth certificates, selling clothing and bedding, and so on. Her rounds of abajo were by no means limited to these monthly visits. Abajo is familiar territory to Carmencita: it is where her sister lives, and where she lived herself before she and her husband acquired a small parcel of land behind La Clarín. She has no trouble negotiating the muddy alleys that twist through abajo, easily locating the shacks of the various people she is visiting and stopping to gossip with friends along the way.

Whereas most of her Dominican counterparts avoid the alleyways of abajo, Carmencita and Digna exhibit bravado and a range of movement more in keeping with Wilson's "reputation." There are many women who are dedicated to working for the community, but few know the barrio as well as Carmencita and Digna. Carmencita enacts toughness and freedom by visiting any part of the barrio she chooses, even in the evening. Her resistance to the barrio's dualism is entirely deliberate. Carmencita likes to point out that although she is small, she is not afraid. Similarly, the Jesuit priests, who themselves are from disparate parts of the country or overseas, also make a point of learning their way around the barrio, and their knowledge often surpasses that of residents.

A couple of years ago, Carmencita gained formal employment in the newly built Catholic Church. She is in charge of the keys and must let in suppliers, make sure the priests' vestments are washed and ready, and keep the church clean. Through her own determination, she has attained a position of security and respectability that suits her very well. Illiteracy and mobility have not stopped Carmencita from commanding respect.

Carmencita, Digna, and the Catholic Church are hardly contesting social hierarchy, yet their practices call into question social stratifications that are objectified onto barrio space. While the church only challenges the state in limited ways, it does deliberately transgress local boundaries, encouraging residents to think beyond their own sector and collaborate in activities such as Thursday Mass, prayer meetings, and community organizations. It is of the state and yet not of the state. Its institutional ambiguity both empowers and confines cienigüeros. As the poor's major institutional resort, it mediates the conditions that maintain both respectability and reputation as prominent forms of value. These contestations of the barrio's moral geography create the basis for a class identity that contests the barrio's stigmatization. While residents engage in a struggle for position within the barrio, they are also forced to acknowledge that they are emplaced and enclassed collectively: the class structure does not distinguish the respectable urban poor from the delincuentes.

THE DOMINICAN TIGER: DELINQUENT OR NATIONAL HERO?

Respectability is not the only institution that comes into question as part of a dualism. Equally as challenging is the tíguere, a liminal character who Christian Krohn-Hansen describes as "a survivor in his environment . . . both an everyday hero and a sort of trickster" (1996, 108–9). However, he or she challenges dualism in a way that is quite different from Adela and Cristino, with their use of reputation to gain respectability, or even Carmencita, who challenges the barrio's spatial dualism in various ways. While, at first glance, the tíguere appears to squarely fit the category of "reputation," closer examination suggests that this character challenges the opposition of respectability and reputation altogether. In this section I will default to using the personal pronoun *he* to discuss the tíguere, to reflect the term's origin as a male archetype, but today the term is just as applicable to women as to men.

Like his feline namesake, the tíguere is strong, cunning, and commands respect. He has positive and negative forms: he is at once admired for his courage and shrewdness, and reviled for his manipulation of others to meet his own ends. At face value, the tíguere seems to correspond very well to Wilson's (1973) category of reputation. Although the type is urban-based, it draws heavily on rural values of masculinity comprising five main features: the rural man must have courage, be visible in the public sphere, be a seducer but also a good father and husband, have excellent oratory skills, and be serious and sincere (Wilson, 1973). These qualities are evident in the urban tíguere, yet many of them are also part of being an hombre de la casa. The primary distinctions between these two male types are their social-networking behaviors and spatial scope: whereas the hombre de la casa associates primarily with his close family and often attends church, the tíguere must be visible on the street and network with other men.

In its positive form, the term *tíguere* is used throughout Dominican society to complement individuals' skills, style, or cunning. For example, if a person makes a good speech, wins a game of dominoes in style, or makes a good deal, then he or she may receive the praise "¡Que tíguere!" meaning "What a tiger!" Krohn-Hansen points out that it may also be used admiringly in reference to a doctor or a minister, and it is increasingly used in relation to women. For example, Steven Gregory relates how a Dominican man described his one-year-old daughter as "mas tíguere" (more tiger-like) than his five-year-old daughter "because she only rarely smiled or cried and seemed to possess a more forceful personality" (2007, 41).

In its negative form, tigüeraje is considered to be close to delincuencia. Tigüeraje is spoken about as a manifestation of crisis due to economic instability and overcrowding in poor neighborhoods. In this rendition, the tíguere is a young man who uses his cunning in crime for individualistic ends. Such young men form gangs who take control of abajo and, in the evening, control the streets throughout the barrio. This negative version of the tíguere is associated with imported goods and clothing from the United States, such as baseball caps and designer shoes. Tígueres embody conspicuous consumption with their motorbikes, latest mobile phones, guns, and well-styled hair. They are marked by their gender (male), age (approximately fifteen to thirty), clothes (brands such as Nike), and masculine accessories (motorbikes and guns).

By spending scarce money on consumer goods, the tíguere may oppose middle-class views that the poor should behave prudently, but his conspicuous consumption is also criticized by his fellow barrio residents. One of Marco's complaints about people who live abajo is that their values are inverted and they exhibit too much tigüeraje: they will spend their money *divertiendose* (enjoying themselves), including buying status symbols such as guns and powerful stereos that mark them out as having reputation, rather than improving their houses and truly progressing. They are condemned for having lost faith in Dominican values, turning to the ephemerality of the street rather than the stability of the household. Thus, individualism and consumption are derided as a loss of traditional values. The problem is generally not consumption per se, but consumption at the expense of practicing normative values.

In everyday practice, however, tigüeraje implies cunning and creativity far more than crime and loss of morality. The tiger is a revealing symbol of the position that many barrio dwellers find themselves in when confronted with a society that is ready to condemn them. Through his knowledge and his toughness, the tíguere has the ability to resist and overcome, two very necessary survival tactics in the barrios of Santo Domingo. Indeed, at times it is deliberately performed for economic benefit. Unable to gain permanent employment, young men may develop the persona of a tíguere to make a living from informal work on the street. Steven Gregory describes how in Boca Chica, a resort town located thirty minutes' drive from Santo Domingo, hustlers struggle to make a living due to the "spatial economy of difference" (2007, 50) that separates tourists and locals, excluding the poor from the profits of the tourist industry. Tourism police patrol the local beaches, ensuring that locals do not enter the zone in front of the hotels unless they are licensed vendors. Hustlers must circumvent these barriers to gain access to tourists and sell them services such as shopping tours or sex. One needs to be streetwise in order to survive.

In La Ciénaga, the motoconchista embodies the liminality of the tíguere. Given the barrio's lack of transport, motoconchistas provide an essential service ferrying passengers from the barrio to the city. They are respectable insofar as they work for a living, but their street work entails the transgression of borders and makes them privy to knowledge of criminal activity. Being a motoconchista is a dangerous job, and it depends on extensive knowledge of the streets and their people. They cannot operate without the consent of other motoconchistas, who jealously guard their occupation from newcomers so as to maintain sufficient clientele. Motoconchistas work out of sites where their friends also work, and support each other in negotiations with passengers. They build up networks along their routes to inform them about what is taking place in the street: whether the police are out booking people with defective bikes, or whether delincuentes have been operating in certain places. Like Gregory's tígueres, the motoconchistas' tigüeraje involves transgressing the borders of moral geographies, simultaneously providing a means of livelihood and a source of danger.

While the figure of the Dominican tíguere seems very close to Wilson's man of reputation, its place in Dominican society has changed significantly over time. Christian Krohn-Hansen writes that the term *tíguere* first appeared among working-class men in Santo Domingo during the 1930s, when Trujillo's tight control necessitated innovative and courageous evasion tactics. Today, however, the figure has lost much of its oppositional edge. It is now so prominent as to become synonymous, in some cases, with Dominican citizenship. The Dominican journalist Lipe Collado, author of *El Tíguere Dominicano* (1992), notes that Dominicans in New York are often collectively referred to as tígueres because they use the phrase so regularly.

The flexibility of the term *tíguere* allows it to cross class and gender boundaries to become a master symbol of Dominican identity. In other words, the Dominican tíguere is a bridge spanning the divide of respectability and reputation. With freedom of movement, conspicuous consumption, and individualized style, it is perhaps of little wonder that the tíguere holds appeal for such a broad range of Dominican society. Packaged up in this masculinized, subversive, yet highly social identity are the potentialities for overcoming the struggles of life and achieving the progress that the Dominican state and its citizens have imagined together.

This, in essence, is the condition of La Ciénaga. Through everyday activities—autoconstruction, engagement with space, dualism, sociality, tigüeraje, respectability, consumption—residents chip away at the problems they face and slowly advance their socioeconomic positions. Neither radical nor overtly political, cienigüeros enact the struggle of the marginal—the "survivor in his environment"—defined by difficulty and the need to *resolver* (solve problems). In so doing, they reproduce the stereotypes and structural inequalities that bind them to place, but they also challenge them in many ways. This is no lightening revolution: radical change does occur in the barrios, but it can take decades or even generations to achieve, and it is by no means a simple task of replacing one dominant ideology with another. Instead, plural meanings and values are objectified onto, and interpreted through, an array of material things that form the stuff of social life. In other words, poverty, marginality, and the values associated with them are relative not just in the present, but also across time and space.

CODA

On January 20, 2011, I flew into Port-au-Prince for the first time. I had visited Haiti previously, accompanying Carmencita when she visited her family in Peredo in 2005, but we had not passed through the capital city. This time, I had come to spend two months working with fellow anthropologists Espelencia Baptiste and Heather Horst to investigate how Haitians were responding to a new system to allow people without bank accounts to send money via mobile phone. It was just over a year since the 7.0 magnitude earthquake that shook Port-au-Prince and Jacmel, and the city was still a mess. Rubble lined the streets, houses perched precariously as they slanted forty degrees toward the ground, and tens of thousands of people were living in makeshift camps. Many houses, substandard to begin with, had sustained structural damage, and for weeks or months after the quake, Haitians and foreign visitors alike slept outside lest an aftershock send their dwelling tumbling down (Farmer 2011). The plight of Americans whose mortgages were foreclosed paled in comparison with this scene of material destruction and loss of life. The poverty of the former is primarily relative; the latter can only be described as abject.

Dominicans, watching from the other side of the island, witnessed the catastrophe on the nightly news, read about it in local newspapers, and heard accounts of experiences from Haitian neighbors. When I visited Santo Domingo directly after my fieldwork in Port-au-Prince, I was trepidatious about what Dominicans would think of the disaster. A vast literature attests to the fact that Dominicans have never responded well to Haitian migrants, deriding their poverty as the result of their "natural" (racialized) characteristics (Corten 1981; Grasmuck 1982; Martínez 1995; 1999). In 2005, I had planned my trip despite my neighbors in La Ciénaga warning me that Haiti was too dangerous to visit. Such were cienigüeros' images of Haiti's poverty that one woman told me that I should take with me all the food that I would need for the trip, because there wasn't any in Haiti. When I returned to La Ciénaga, I was pleased to be able to show my friends photos of Haiti and hear their exclamations of surprise, such as "There are trees in Haiti!" and "It's just like the countryside here!" Somehow, living alongside Haitians for decades had not sufficed to dispel the idea that Haiti was a different world altogether. Nor did the fact that their own barrio was stigmatized as a place where one would be "murdered for your shoes" cause them to stop and think that perhaps the Dominican fear of Haiti was based more on myth than reality. I wondered whether the earthquake had cemented their views of Haiti's abjection, and possibly also their negative moral judgments of Haitians.

In 2011, I returned to the Dominican Republic fearing a fresh round of antihaitianismo. The earthquake had brought a new wave of Haitians who wanted to escape from the toppled city where they had seen loved ones pass away in front of their eyes, and I had heard of various incidents in which Haitian refugees from the earthquake had been met with hostility by their reluctant Dominican hosts. To my surprise and relief, I met person after person who expressed empathy with the plight of Haitians. They were horrified by the catastrophe, and proudly reported to me that their government had been the first to step in and help their Hispaniolan neighbors. I saw an increasing amount of political graffiti around Santo Domingo calling for the two halves of the island to unite, a sentiment that would have been almost universally rejected just a few years ago. Of course, these altered sentiments by no means indicate a complete reversal of antihaitianismo: the help offered by the Dominican state was accompanied by a new wave of discrimination, including restricting border migration and denying citizenship to Haitians born in the Dominican Republic. Nevertheless, the shift in attitudes that I and others have witnessed was significant, and it should be taken seriously as a sign that the transformation of values does indeed occur.

I wondered what had precipitated such a sudden change in attitude in the face of a history of antihaitianismo. If Dominicans derided Haitians for their poverty before, why were they sympathetic now? After talking with various people and hearing what they had to say, I surmised that cienigüeros' increased sympathies lay partly in how the earthquake made poverty real. Decidedly not an everyday event, the earthquake prompted value reassessments of a kind that generally take years to form. Before the earthquake, Dominicans tended to view Haitian poverty as attributable to a faulty Haitian character, which permitted environmental destruction, violence, and national disorder. After the earthquake, Haitian poverty changed in the eyes of (at least some) Dominicans. With such a loss of life, and risk of further bodily harm from lack of shelter and diseases, Haitian poverty took on an abject quality. The earthquake demonstrated how, of all social groups, the poor are in the greatest danger of slipping from survival into abjection, for reasons that are natural or structural, rather than of their own making.

Upon reflection, however, I do not think that this shift in Dominican attitudes was solely attributable to the scale of the catastrophe and loss of life, nor was it as sudden as it seemed. For a few decades now, a black consciousness movement and women's movement have been growing in the Dominican Republic (Cassá 1995). There is a greater awareness of racism across the board, possibly as migration and media bring alternative visions home. In the eight years that I have been visiting Santo Domingo, far more has changed than the material appearance of the city. An increasing number of young Dominican women braid their hair or wear hair nets, practices that used to be scorned as Haitian and undesirable. My good friend Yoselyn is no longer unusual in her consistent refusal to straighten her beautiful curls, and Afros are also now fashionable among youth. I remember Carmencita remarking to me in 2005 that economic crisis had forced Dominicans to adopt Haitian cultural practices:

> Before, Haitians had no value; if you lived here they treated you like a rag because you weren't in your own country. They used to say that arrenque, black beans, cornflower, capique, and sardines were Haitian foods. They didn't eat these things. Bananas were Haitian food. Now there are vitamins in them! Maize flour, arrenque is vitamin and nourishing, all this nourishes. Before if you ate this you must be

Haitian, but now, ooh! Now these foods are tasty for them because
things are bad everywhere.

In other words, tastes have changed in response to circumstance. However, we could postulate that economic growth, as much as crisis, has
prompted this shift. It is equally possible that Dominicans, feeling more
secure and having witnessed concrete signs of change, feel less precarious in their abilities to carve out a livelihood and therefore less pressure
to differentiate themselves from others according to a "spatial economy
of difference" (Gregory 2007).

Based on my observations of La Ciénaga's transformation, I would
say that feelings of greater security that accompany economic growth
and material improvement have prompted a shift in attitudes across the
board. Over the past eight years I have watched as the barrio's housing
stock has changed, public spaces have been redeveloped, and entrepreneurs have set up new businesses, such as small supermarkets and
Internet cafés. I have also witnessed a distinct reduction in the stigmatization of the barrio by outsiders, and far less antagonism between residents of La Ciénaga. No longer so afraid of crime, and feeling more
secure in their present material condition (though often still trepidatious about the future), cienigüeros are less motivated to find fault with
each other. Reduced precarity means that they can spend more energy
practicing one key Dominican value in particular: sociality. The barrios
in particular are well-placed to enact this value, because the built environment that results from autoconstruction facilitates everyday contact
between family members and neighbors. They also benefit from sociality in a material sense as cooperation helps them to resolve, or bypass,
the problems that their poverty confers.

It is currently too early to say for sure which direction Dominican-
Haitian relations will head, or what the future holds for Santo Domingo's poor. However, these signs of change are a reminder that social
values alter along with material fortunes. In the main, values shift not in
response to rapid change (such as a revolution), but as an outcome of
the everyday activities of masses of people over a long period of time.
This is why individual- or household-centered strategies for progress,
such as autoconstruction, have transformative power. What began as a
quest by individual families to carve out living space has resulted in La
Ciénaga being incorporated into the public life of the city and the

jurisdiction of the state. The evidence they put forward was their very materiality: not only were they too many to ignore, so that the state could not move them on, but also transforming their homes into concrete, and their barrio into an urban community, gave them a permanence of place and belonging that a shack in a swamp does not.

This permanence is symbolic as well as practical: in making place themselves, residents have demonstrated their commitment to the core values of family and home, and therefore also their own suitability to be incorporated into the city's formal structures. This adherence to normative national values can be seen as oppositional in that it reflects the efforts of the poor to be admitted to the realms of urban citizenship. They have fought against a politics of *mis*-recognition (see C. Taylor 1994; E. B. Taylor 2010) that moralizes their poverty, and seeks to demoralize them as social beings. Autoconstruction, which began with an economic imperative, thereby entails a range of social effects that cannot be easily classified as "resistance" or "domination." Within two generations, squatters in Santo Domingo's barrios have significantly altered their own life circumstances through their material labors and creative designs. They have been enabled to do so by the very constraints that bind them to place.

Yet we are also left with the question of what kinds of transformations these everyday strategies produce. In La Ciénaga, change has been radical, but it has also been conservative. A material project that developed under the radar of the state, and was made concrete by the sweat and dreams of residents, has ended up leading back to the state after all, as residents literally built themselves into the city and demanded their rights as urban residents. As the relationship between the Dominican Republic and Haiti demonstrates, the state has its own ideological projects, realized through physical and structural violence, that are entrenched in bureaucratic processes. History becomes objectified in more or less permanent institutions, and these can be slow to change. One positive recent sign is the removal of racial identifiers from Dominican national identity cards, signalling a shift to greater bureaucratic equality for Dominican citizens. However, documentation, national borders, the distribution of resources, and the mobilization of police are just some of the mechanisms by which the state exerts power in asymmetric ways. While barrio residents can achieve an impressive array of transformation of their own material situation, the role of material things in the practice of state power is also worth examination.

A polyvalent understanding of how material forms are implicated in social stratification can help us understand a great deal more than experiences of poverty around the world. Materiality is not just central to the lives and coping strategies of poor people. It also illustrates a general truth about contemporary life: that no matter how hard we try to escape or downplay the materiality of the world, whether through the creation of virtual online worlds or the abstraction of the economy, our society and economy are founded on actual, concrete things, and social changes are founded on our daily interactions with them. Our tendency to forget this, or abstract it, is part of what obfuscates how social stratification is produced, reproduced, and overcome. Understanding better the materiality of power, realized through everyday actions of individuals, communities, and institutions, can assist in tracing chains of cause and consequence in the maintenance of the status quo or the transformation of lives.

GLOSSARY

abajo el puente: under the bridge

abajo: below, used to refer to the barrios in the flood lands of the Ozama River or the low parts of La Ciénaga

agua negra: black water

antihaitianismo: anti-Haitianism

arriba: above, used to refer to the majority of Santo Domingo or the high parts of La Ciénaga

bala perdida: stray bullet

barrio caliente: hot barrio

barrio marginado: marginal neighborhood

Barrio Seguro: Safe Barrio, a police program to increase security in the barrios

barrio: neighborhood, usually poor

blanco: white, a racial category

bulla: noise, uproar

café dulce: sweet coffee

caliente: hot, troublesome

calle: street

callejón: alley

camino bueno: good path

campo: countryside, field

cañanda: gulley, canal, stormwater drain

capitaleño: resident of the capital city of Santo Domingo

casa buena: good house

caudillo: political strongman

CES: Centro de Estudios Sociales Padre Angelo Montalvo (The Father Angelo Montalvo Social Studies Center)

chiripero: street vending or odd jobs

cienigüeros: residents of La Ciénaga

clase media: middle class

CODECI: Comité para el Desarrollo de La Ciénaga (Committee for the Development of La Ciénaga)

colmado: small grocery store

colmadón: grocery store with a bar

comedor: food stall or small restaurant

COPADEBA: Comité Popular para la Defensa de los Barrios (Popular Committee for the Defense of the Barrios)

corrupción: corruption, meaning moral weakness

culto: lit. cult, but refers to a religious sermon

delincuente: delinquent

desalojo: eviction

dominicanidad: Dominicanness

ensanche: widening, referring to a particular type of planned neighborhood

¡E'pa'lante que vamos!: It's forward we go!

gente de trabajo: working people

gente seria: serious people

hablando vaina: speaking rubbish, gossiping

hombre de la casa: man of the house

IFZ: Industrial Free Zone, zona franca

IMF: International Monetary Fund

indio: Indian, a racial category

Junta de Vecinos: Neighborhood Council

la ciénaga: the swamp

La Clarín: The Radio Tower, referring to a part of La Ciénaga

la dominicana: The Dominican Republic

la mano dura: strong hand

¡llegó la luz!: The light arrived!

luchar: struggle

malecón: waterfront

marido: common-law husband

monte: wilderness

moreno: brown, a racial category

motoconchista: motorbike taxi driver

movimiento: movement

mujer sin vergüenza: shameless woman

negro: black, a racial category

para adelante: onward, forward

PLD: Partido de la Liberación Dominicana (Dominican Liberation Party)

pobre: poor

PRD: Partido Revolucionario Dominicano (Dominican Revolutionary Party)

prieto: pitch black, a racial category

ranchito: small house made of wood and/or tin

residencial: planned neighborhood

resolver: resolve problems

tigüeraje: streetwise behavior

tíguere: [sic] tiger, streetwise person

trabajando para la comunidad: working for the community

tranquilidad: tranquility, peacefulness

vaina: sheath, especially of a bean; used to mean "rubbish," a common Dominican expression

zona colonial: colonial zone

zona turistica: tourism zone

REFERENCES

Abel, Joshua, and Joseph Tracey. 2012. "The Changing Face of Foreclosures." *Liberty Street Economics*, March 21.

Amnesty International. 2000. *Dominican Republic: Killings by Security Forces*. Accessed July 9, 2013, from www.amnesty.org/en/library/asset/AMR27/001/2000/en/dfe5e3cd-de09-11dd-a3e1-93acb0aa12d8/amr270012000en.pdf.

Andrade, Manuel J. 1969. *Folklore from the Dominican Republic*. New York: Kraus Reprint.

Austin, Diane J. 1981. "Born Again . . . and Again and Again: Communitas and Social Change among Jamaican Pentecostalists." *Journal of Anthropological Research* 37(3):226–46.

———. 1983. "Culture and Ideology in the English-Speaking Caribbean: A View from Jamaica." *American Ethnologist* 10:223–40.

———. 1984. *Urban Life in Kingston, Jamaica*. New York: Gordon and Breach.

Austin-Broos, Diane J. 1997. *Jamaica Genesis: Religion and the Politics of Moral Orders*. Chicago: The University of Chicago Press.

———. 2009. *Arrernte Present, Arrernte Past: Invasion, Violence and Imagination in Indigenous Central Australia*. Chicago and London: University of Chicago Press.

Berman, Marshall. 1982. *All That Is Solid Melts into Air*. New York and London: Penguin Books.

Betances, Emilio. 2007. *The Catholic Church and Power Politics in Latin America: The Dominican Case in Comparative Perspective*. Lanham, MD: Rowman & Littlefield.

Birdwell-Pheasant, Donna, and Denise Lawrence-Zuñiga. 1999. *House Life: Space, Place and Family in Europe*. Oxford and New York: Berg.

Bosch, Juan. 1992. *Clases sociales en la República Dominicana*. Santo Domingo: Editora Corripio.

Bourdieu, Pierre. 1970. "The Berber House or the World Reversed." *Social Science Information* 9(2):151–70.

———. 1984. *Distinction: A Social Critique of the Judgement of Taste*. Cambridge: Harvard University Press.

———. 1986. "The Forms of Capital." In *Handbook of Theory and Research for the Sociology of Education*, edited by John G. Richardso n, 241–58. Westport, CT: Greenwood Press.

Briceño-León, Roberto, and Verónica Zubillaga. 2002. "Violence and Globalization in Latin America." *Current Sociology* 50(1):19–37.

Caldeira, Teresa. 2000. *City of Walls: Crime, Segregation, and Citizenship in Sao Paulo*. Berkeley: University of California Press.

Candelario, Ginetta. 2007. *Black behind the Ears: Dominican Racial Identity from Museums to Beauty Shops*. Durham and London: Duke University Press.

Carey, Nick. 2012. "Americans Brace for Next Foreclosure Wave." *Reuters*, April 4. Accessed July 9, 2013, from www.reuters.com/article/2012/04/04/us-foreclosure-idUSBRE83319E20120404.

Cassá, Roberto. 1995. "Recent Popular Movements in the Dominican Republic." *Latin American Perspectives* 86:80–93.

Cela, Jorge. 1997. *La otra cara de la pobreza*. Santo Domingo: Centro de Estudios Sociales Padre Juan Montalvo.

CES. 2004. *Agenda de trabajo para el desarrollo barrial: La Ciénaga*. Santo Domingo: Centro de Estudios Sociales P adre Juan Montalvo.

Collado, Lipe. 1992. *El tíguere dominicano*. Santo Domingo: Panamericana.

Comaroff, Jean, and John L. Comaroff. 2001. "Millennial Capitalism: First Thoughts on a Second Coming." In *Millennial Capitalism and the Culture of Neoliberalism*, edited by Jean Comaroff and John L. Comaroff, 1–56. Durham and London: Duke University Press.

Corten, Andre. 1981. "The Migration of Haitian Workers to Sugar Factories in the Dominican Republic." In *Contemporary Caribbean: A Sociological Reader*, edited by Susan Craig, 349–81. Maracas, Trinidad and Tobago: The College Press.

Crousset, Carol. 2004. "Guachupita, en estado de emergencia: dos muertos y nueve heridos en 5 días." *El Caribe*, October 1.

Davis, Mike. 2006. *Planet of Slums*. London: Verso.

Derby, Lauren. 1998. *The Magic of Modernity: Dictatorship and Civic Culture in the Dominican Republic, 1916–1962*. PhD dissertation, the University of Chicago.

———. 2003. "Race, National Identity and the Idea of Value on the Island of Hispaniola." In *Blacks, Coloreds and National Identity in Nineteenth-Century Latin America*, edited by Nancy P. Naro, 5–37. London: Institute of Latin American Studies, University of London.

———. 2009. *The Dictator's Seduction: Politics and the Popular Imagination in the Era of Trujillo*. Durham and London: Duke University Press.

Dore y Cabral, Carlos. 1981. *The Eastern Situation and Agrarian Reform in the Dominican Republic*. Maracas, Trinidad and Tobago: The College Press.

Douglas, Mary L., and Baron C. Isherwood. 1978. *The World of Goods: Towards an Anthropology of Consumption*. New York City: W.W. Norton.

El Caribe. 2004. "Homicidios crecieron 60% en esta década según el informe de la PN presentado al Congreso." *El Caribe*, March 2 .

Engels, Friedrich. 1987 [1887]. "The Condition of the Working Class in England." Harmondsworth, Middlesex: Penguin.

Farmer, Paul. 1997. "On Suffering and Structural Violence: A View from Below." In *Social Suffering*, edited by Arthur Kleinman, Veena Das, and Margaret Lock, 261–83. Berkeley and Los Angeles: University of California Press.

Farmer, Paul. 2011. *Haiti After the Earthquake*. New York: Public Affairs.

———. 2004. "An Anthropology of Structural Violence." *Current Anthropology* 45(3):305–25.

Fay, Marianne, and Anna Wellenstein. 2005. "Keeping a Roof over One's Head: Improving Access to Safe and Decent Shelter." In *The Urban Poor in Latin America*, edited by Marianne Fay, 91–124. Washington, DC: The World Bank.

Fay, Marianne, and Caterina Ruggeri Laderchi. 2005. "Urban Poverty in Latin America and the Caribbean: Setting the Stage." In *The Urban Poor in Latin America*, edited by Marianne Fay, 19–46. Washington, DC: The World Bank.

Ferguson, James. 1992. *The Dominican Republic: Beyond the Lighthouse*. London: Latin America Bureau.

———. 1993. "Pain and Protest: The 1984 Anti-IMF Revolt in the Dominican Republic." In *Caribbean Freedom: Economy and Society from Emancipation to the Present*, edited by Hilary Beckles and Verene Shepherd, 566–74. Kingston, Jamaica: I. Randle Publishers; London: J. Curry Publishers.

García, Genris. 1995a. "Enfrentamientos La Ciénaga dejan heridos y detenidos." *El Siglo*, March 11.

———. 1995b. "Darían 50 viviendas a familias La Ciénaga." *El Siglo*, March 14 .

———. 1997. "La Ciénaga y Los Guandules libran lucha en dos frentes quieren g obierno concluya obras y PN acabe delincuencia." *El Siglo*, June 26.

Gautreaux Piñeyro, Bonaparte. 2005. "Abrir las puertas." *Hoy*, March 6.

Geertz, Clifford. 1973. *The Interpretation of Cultures: Selected Essays*. Fontana, CA: Fontana.

Goode, Erich, and Nachmann Ben-Yehuda. 1994. *Moral Panics: The Social Construction of Deviance*. Oxford, UK, and Cambridge, MA: Blackwell.

Grasmuck, Sherri. 1982. "Migration within the Periphery: Haitian Labor in the Dominican Sugar and Coffee Industries." *International Migration Review* 16:365–77.

Grasmuck, Sherri, and Patricia R. Pessar. 1991. *Between Two Islands: Dominican International Migration*. Berkeley and Los Angeles: University of California Press.

Gregory, Steven. 2007. *The Devil behind the Mirror: Globalization and Politics in the Dominican Republic*. Berkeley and Los Angeles: University of California Press.

Harré, Rom. 2002. "Material Objects in Social Worlds." *Theory, Culture, Society* 19:23–33.

Harvey, David. 1989. *The Condition of Postmodernity*. Oxford: Basil Blackwell Ltd.

———. 2000. "Cosmopolitanism and the Banality of Geographical Evils." *Public Culture* 12(2):529–64.

Hoffnung-Garskof, Jesse. 2008. *A Tale of Two Cities: Santo Domingo and New York after 1950*. Princeton and Oxford: Princeton University Press.

Holston, James. 1991. "Autoconstruction in Working-Class Brazil." *Cultural Anthropology* 6:447–65.

Horst, Heather, and Daniel Miller. 2006. *The Cell Phone: An Anthropology of Communication*. New York: Berg.

Howard, David. 2001. *Coloring the Nation: Race and Ethnicity in the Dominican Republic*. Oxford: Signal Books.

Human Rights Watch. 2002. "'Illegal People': Haitians and Dominico-Haitians in the Dominican Republic." *Human Rights Watch* 14:1–32.

Ireland, Rowan. 1993. "The Crentes of Campo Alegre and the Religious Construction of Brazilian Politics." In *Rethinking Protestantism in Latin America*, edited by Virginia Garrard Burnett and David Stoll, 45–65. Philadelphia: Temple University Press.

Jameson, Fredric. 1998. "Notes on Globalization as a Philosophical Issue." In *The Cultures of Globalization*, edited by Fredric Jameson and Masao Miyoshi, 54–77. Durham and London: Duke University Press.

———. 2005. *Archaeologies of the Future: The Desire Called Utopia and Other Science Fictions*. London and New York: Verso.

Khan, Aisha. 2004. *Callaloo Nation: Metaphors of Race and Religious Identity among South Asians in Trinidad*. Durham and London: Duke University Press.

Kleinman, Arthur, Veena Das, and Margaret Lock. 1997. *Social Suffering*. Berkeley and Los Angeles: University of California Press.

Knight, Franklin W. 1990. *The Caribbean: The Genesis of a Fragmented Nationalism* (2nd ed.). New York: Oxford University Press.

Krohn-Hansen, Christian. 1996. "Masculinity and the Political among Dominicans: 'The Dominican Tiger.'" In *Machos, Mistresses, Madonnas: Contesting the Power of Latin American Gender Imagery*, edited by Marit Melhuus and Kristi Anne Stølen, 108–33. London and New York: Verso.

———. 2001. "A Tomb for Columbus in Santo Domingo: Political Cosmology, Population and Racial Frontiers." *Social Anthropology* 9:165–92.

Levine, Daniel H. 1992. *Popular Voices in Latin American Catholicism*. Princeton, NJ: Princeton University Press.

Malinowski, Bronislaw. 1922. *Argonauts of the Western Pacific*. New York: Dutton.

Martínez, Samuel. 1995. *Peripheral Migrants: Haitians and Dominican Republic Sugar Plantations*. Knoxville: University of Tennessee Press.

———. 1999. "From Hidden Hand to Heavy Hand: Sugar, the State, and Migrant Labor in Haiti and the Dominican Republic." *Latin American Research Review* 34(1):57–84.

Martínez-Vergne, Teresita. 2005. *Nation and Citizen in the Dominican Republic, 1880–1916*. Chapel Hill: The University of North Carolina Press.

Medrano, Freddy, and Pedro Martínez. 1997. "Muere joven herido protesta La Ciénaga." *La Noticia*, January 29.

Miller, Daniel. 1987. *Material Culture and Mass Consumption*. Oxford, UK, and Cambridge, MA: Blackwell.

———. 1994. *Modernity: An Ethnographic Approach: Dualism and Mass Consumption in Trinidad*. Providence, RI, and Oxford, UK: Berg.

———. 2001. "The Poverty of Morality." *Journal of Consumer Culture* 1(2):225–43.

———. 2008. *The Comfort of Things*. Cambridge: Polity Press.

Ministry of Rural Development. 2011. *Socio-economic and Caste Census Begins*. Press Information Bureau, Government of India, June 29. Accessed July 9, 2013, from http://pib.nic.in/newsite/erelease.aspx?relid=72924.

Mintz, Sidney W., and Sally Price (eds.). 1985. *Caribbean Contours*. Baltimore and London: The John Hopkins University Press.

Munn, Nancy D. 1996. "Excluded Spaces: The Figure in the Australian Aboriginal Landscape." *Critical Inquiry* 22(3):446–65.

Myers, Fred. 2002. *Painting Culture: The Making of an Aboriginal High Art*. Durham and London: Duke University Press.

Navarro, Andrés. 2004. *Plan Cigua: Plan de desarrollo urbano para La Ciénaga y Los Guandules*. Santo Domingo: Ciudad Alternativa and CODECIGUA.

Nettleford, Rex. 1971. "Caribbean Perspectives: The Creative Potential and the Quality of Life." *Caribbean Quarterly* 17(3/4):114– 27.

Nuevo Diario. 1997. "El Presidente en los barrios." December 29.

Peña, Oscar. 1997. "Inauguran obras remodelación La Ciénaga." *El Nacional*, August 15.

Pérez Reyes, Ramón. 2005. "Los delincuentes le quitaron la paz y tranquilidad a Gazcue." *Listín Diario*, February 10.

Perlman, Janice E. 1976. *The Myth of Marginality: Urban Poverty and Politics in Rio de Janeiro*. Berkeley and Los Angeles: University of California Press.

———. 2003. "Marginality: From Myth to Reality in the Favelas of Rio de Janeiro, 1969–2002." In *Urban Informality: Transnational Perspectives from the Middle East, Latin America, and South Asia*, edited by Ananya Roy and Nezar Alsayyad , 105–46. Lanham, MD: Lexington Books.

Portes, Alejandro, Carlos Dore-Cabral, and Patricia Landlolt (eds.). 1997. *The Urban Caribbean: Transition to the New Global Economy*. Baltimore and London: The John Hopkins University Press.

Prown, Jules D. 1982. "Mind in Matter: An Introduction to Material Culture Theory and Method." *Witherfur Portfolio* 17(1):1–19.

Ramírez, Leonora. 2005. "En cinco años, 1,376 asesinatos 'extrajudiciales.'" *Hoy*, March 2.

Rámos, Ana Maria. 1996. "13 mil familias viven hacinadas en La Ciénaga." *Hoy*, September 4.

Richard, François G. 2011. "Materializing Poverty: Archaeological Reflections from the Postcolony." *Historical Archaeology* 45(3):166–82.

Robotham, Donald. 2005. *Culture, Society and Economy: Bringing Production Back In*. London: Sage Publications.

Rugh, Jacob S., and Douglas S. Massey. 2010. "Racial Segregation and the American Foreclosure Crisis." *American Sociological Review* 75(5):629–51.

Ruiz Matuk, Ellias. 2005. "Han muerto 333 en 'intercambios.'" *Hoy*, July 17.

Sáez, José L. 2007. *El Quehacer de la Iglesia Dominicana (1511–2006)*. Santo Domingo: Centro Fe y Cultura Roberto Bellamino.

Safa, Helen I. 1995. *The Myth of the Male Breadwinner: Women and Industrialization in the Caribbean*. Boulder, CO: Westview Press.

Sagás, Ernesto. 2000. *Race and Politics in the Dominican Republic*. Gainesville: University Press of Florida.

Sahlins, Marshall. 1972. *Stone Age Economics*. Chicago: Aldine-Atherton.

———. 1991. "La Pensée Bourgeoise: Western Society as Culture." In *Rethinking Popular Culture: Contempory Perspectives in Cultural Studies*, edited by Chandra Mukerji and Michael Schudson, 166–221. Berkeley and Los Angeles: University of California Press.

Santana, Julio. 2004. *Zona Norte: La expulsión de los excluidos*. Santo Domingo: Ciudad Alternativa.

Scheper-Hughes, Nancy. 1992. *Death without Weeping: The Violence of Everyday Life in Brazil*. Berkeley and Los Angeles: University of California Press.

Sen, Amartya. 1999. *Development as Freedom*. Oxford: Oxford University Press.

Shepherd, Frederick M. 1993. "Church and State in Honduras and Nicaragua Prior to 1979." *Sociology of Religion* 54(3):277–93.

Taylor, Charles. 1994. *Multiculturalism: Examining the Politics of Recognition*. Princeton, NJ: Princeton University Press.

Taylor, Erin B. 2009a. "From *el campo* to *el barrio* : Memory and Social Imaginaries in Santo Domingo." *Identities: Global Studies in Culture and Power* 16(2):157–78.

———. 2009b. "Poverty as Danger: Fear of Crime in Santo Domingo." *International Journal of Cultural Studies* 12(2):35–52.

———. 2010. "A Reluctant Locality: The Politics of Place and Progress." In *Making Locals: Migration and the Micropolitics of Place*, edited by Catherine Trundle and Brigitte Boenisch-Brednich, 101–17. Surrey, UK: Ashgate.

Tejeda, Raul. 2000. *La Ciénaga y Los Guandules: Características socio-económicas y demográficas*. Santo Domingo: Ciudad Alternativa y Plan Cigua.

Tett, Gillian. 2009. *Fool's Gold: How the Bold Dream of a Small Tribe at J.P. Morgan was Corrupted by Wall Street Greed and Unleashed a Catastrophe*. New York: Free Press.

Thompson, David. 2012. "Cosmopolitanism Sits in Places: Consumption and Cosmopolitics in Latin America." *International Review of Social Research* 2 (3): 59–77.

Torres-Saillant, Silvio. 1998. "The Tribulations of Blackness: Stages in Dominican Racial Identity." *Latin American Perspectives* 25 (3): 126–46.

Trouillot, Michel-Rolph. 1995. *Silencing the Past: Power and the Production of History*. Boston: Beacon Press.

United Nations High Commissioner for Refugees. 2010. Report on International Religious Freedom: Dominican Republic. Accessed July 9, 2013, from www.refworld.org/cgi-bin/texis/vtx/rwmain?page=country&category=&publisher=&type=&coi=DOM&rid=4562d94e2&docid=4cf2d0a087&skip=0.

Valenzuela, Angel. 1997. "PN envía a consejo de guerra agente mata joven La Ciénaga." *El Nacional*, February 6.

Vallier, Ivan. 1971. "The Roman Catholic Church: A Transnational Actor." *International Organization* 25(3): 479–502.

Vargas Llosa, Mario. 2000. *La Fiesta del Chivo*. Madrid: Alfaguara.

Vásquez, Manuel. 1999. Toward a New Agenda for the Study of Religion in the Americas. *Journal of Interamerican Studies and World Affairs* 41(4):1–20.

———. 2011. *More Than Belief: A Materialist Theory of Religion*. Oxford: Oxford University Press.

Vicioso, Sherezada. 2000. "Dominicanyorkness: A Metropolitan Discovery of the Triangle." *Callaloo* 23(2):1013–16.

Weiner, Annette B. 1992. *Inalienable Possessions: The Paradox of Keeping-While-Giving*. Berkeley and Los Angeles: University of California Press.

Wilson, Peter. 1973. *Crab Antics: The Social Anthropology of English-Speaking Negro Societies of the Caribbean*. New Haven and London: Yale University Press.

Wolf, Eric R. 1967. Caudillo Politics: A Structural Analysis. *Comparative Studies in Society and History* 9:168–79.

Wolff, Kurt H. 1950. *The Sociology of Georg Simmel*. New York and London: The Free Press.

Wooding, Bridget, and Richard D. Moseley-Williams. 2004. *Needed but Unwanted: Haitian Immigrants and Their Descendants in the Dominican Republic*. London: Catholic Institute for International Relations.

Woodward, Sophie. 2007. *Why Women Wear What They Wear*. Oxford: Berg.

World Bank. 2013. The Dominican Republic. Accessed May 13, 2013, from www.worldbank.org/en/country/dominicanrepublic/overview.

Worsely, Peter. 1968. *The Trumpet Shall Sound: A Study of "Cargo" Cults in Melanesia.* New York: Schocken Books.

INDEX

ABOUT THE AUTHOR

Erin B. Taylor is an Australian anthropologist who is fascinated by the relationships that humans have with each other through material things and money. She received her PhD from the University of Sydney in 2009 and lectured there for three years before taking up a research fellowship at the University of Lisbon. During this time, she helped found the popular anthropology website PopAnth: Hot Buttered Humanity.

Erin's research crisscrosses Hispaniola. On the Dominican-Haitian border, she examined how material culture is implicated in the construction of cultural differences between the two nations. In Haiti she worked on a collaborative project investigating domestic remittances, mobile phone use, and the rollout of a new mobile money system. Objects from this research are featured in the British Museum's Citi Money Gallery.